WOODTURNING

STEP-BY-STEP TECHNIQUES

Oliver Plant

The Crowood Press

First published in 1992 by
The Crowood Press Ltd
Ramsbury, Marlborough
Wiltshire SN8 2HR

British Library Cataloguing in Publication Data

A catalogue record for this book is available from the British
Library.

ISBN 1 85223 584 5

Acknowledgements

The author acknowledges the assistance given by the
following in generously providing literature and information
which has proved invaluable in setting out both the text and
illustrations.

The Axminster Power Tool Centre, Ashley Isles Ltd, Kity UK,
Startrite Heckmondwike, Henry Taylor Tools, Luna Tools &
Machinery Ltd, Multistar Colchester, De Walt Woodworking
Machines, Myford Ltd, Record Power Ltd Sheffield, Craft
Supplies Ltd, John Boddy Ltd, The Woodworker, The Lion
Tool Co Ltd, Hattersley & Davidson Ltd, Rawdon Machine
Sales, Lennartsfors Arjang Sweden; Reading University; Rudolf
Muller, Gmbh Köln; Tom Pettit FRSA MRST; Unwin Hyman;
Dover Publications Inc.; *Practical Woodworking* magazine.

Line illustrations by Noël Trimmer

Typeset by Avonset, Midsomer Norton, Bath
Printed and bound in Great Britain by BPCC Hazells Ltd

CONTENTS

Welcome to one of the most absorbing and satisfying hobbies which, unlike most, can be made to pay for itself – woodturning. I know that it is not easy to learn woodturning from a book as so many of the books on the subject seem to contradict each other, and the advice given is hard to follow. This book takes a new approach to woodturning instruction in that there is as much illustration as there is written content. The illustrations given will, I hope, be clearer than photographs, either in black and white or in colour.

The early part of the book is based upon the two-day beginners' course which I run at Hartford Barton and it should be viewed by the beginner as a refresher to this type of short course, since one cannot hope to remember every detail that has been studied over such an intensive period. It may also be of interest to the more experienced turner, in that there are explained forty-five projects, from thimbles to tapestry frames, which are intended to provide a progression from elementary to advanced work.

The reader will, I think, gain the best benefit from this book by reading from the beginning and continuing through, rather than dipping in where he finds something that takes his interest. The various examples are intended to be part of a progressive learning process and taking some items at random in the last half of the book might lead to problems.

Every woodturner has his own ideas on tools and techniques. This probably arises from the fact that there are so many turning tools which can do the same job (there are at least four different tools that can adequately turn a wooden bead). It is not a hobby in which one can be at all dogmatic; if you find that the tool you wish to use for the job gives you the correct quality and speed of woodturning, then that is the tool for you. The tools I illustrate and suggest for use, the angles to which they have been sharpened, and their method of sharpening,

produce the speed and quality I need. Perhaps more importantly, they are the ones with which my students can readily produce equally good work in quick time.

The reader will notice that imperial measurements are used throughout the book. The reason for this is that you cannot, in the UK at the moment, buy metric turning tools. The reader will also soon become aware of my bias towards large tools. Whilst these can, at first, look daunting to the beginner, my experience is that the average novice gets used to handling a 1½in roughing gouge and, discovering that it allows firm handling and minimum vibration, soon will not use anything else.

There is no substitute for a short course as an introduction to woodturning, mainly because neither a book nor a video can tell the beginner what he has done wrong when suddenly the gouge goes out of control. Only the eye and advice of an experienced woodturner beside him at the time can correct this. The printed notes given to the beginners on my course are reproduced as an appendix to this book which may be found useful as an *aide-memoire* for the novice. As many different kinds of chuck as possible have been used throughout the book in order that their use and capabilities are understood. However, they should not be looked upon as essential pieces of equipment; a lot of very good work can be done on a screw chuck and faceplate when combined with ingenuity and double-sided tape.

In every book on woodturning which I have read there is at least one idea of which I can honestly say 'Good heavens, I hadn't thought of that', and I hope that you, if already experienced in woodturning, will say the same of this book. If a novice then I hope that the new presentation of illustrations throughout and the very large number of examples to be worked will help you on your way to longer shavings and finer finishes.

The Indian Lathe In general use in that country up until 1900, the Indian Lathe is the probable starting point of turning. The lathe required an assistant to provide the motive power and the turner had very few tools other than those shown in the illustration. Note that the handles had to be very long to accommodate his sitting position. The lathe was portable and was taken by the turner and his assistant to wherever the customer required the job to be done.

The Pole Lathe This is not the portable lathe of the bodgers of the beech coppices of High Wycombe, but a more robust model dating from around 1700. It is interesting to note that the pole above the machine was sometimes referred to as a 'lath' and it is thought that this is the origin of the word 'lathe'.

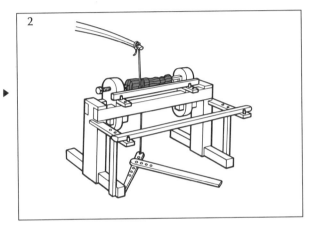

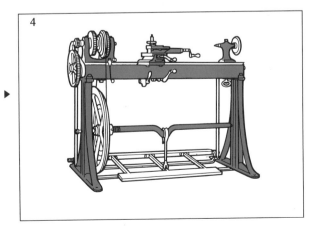

The Treadle Lathe This provided constant rotation in one direction and permitted variation in turning speeds. The frame of the lathe is made of wood which provided a quiet working environment and less vibration than that produced by an iron frame.

Ornamental Turning The Holtzapffel Slide Foot Lathe shown here is used for ornamental turning with the slide rest as fitted, but it can also be used for simple turning with a conventional T-rest. Constructed of iron castings the lathe was popular in the latter half of the nineteenth century for its production of intricate turnings, using a very large number of special attachments.

The Union Graduate This is a heavy and robust lathe much liked by schools since all moving parts of the motor drive are enclosed. The machine can be fitted with either a single- or three-phase motor and has robust headstock bearings and heavy castings which reduce vibration to a minimum. Shown here in its long-bed version, it is also available as a short-bed lathe.

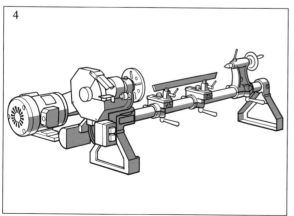

The Tyme Avon Lathe This is shown here as a twin bedbar swinging-head lathe in three-quarter horse-power single-phase. It is a versatile machine available with various lengths between centres.

The Myford Mystro This was first demonstrated at the Woodworker Show at Wembley in 1990. It has a three-quarter horsepower enclosed motor of either single- or three-phase supply. The lathe can be of either standard (40in) or short (12½in) bed lengths. The motor is reversible with five speeds ranging from 350 to 2,400r.p.m. The swing over the bowl turning attachment allows a 20in diameter bowl to be turned.

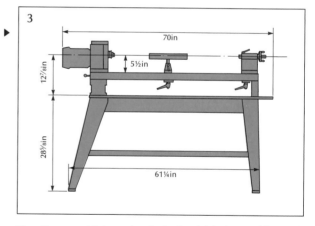

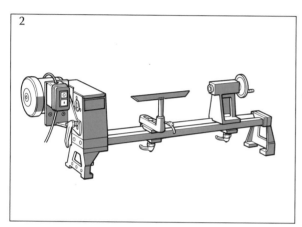

The Coronet Major A relatively old-fashioned but still very popular lathe, with either a three-quarter or one horsepower single-phase motor. The swinging head permits 24in diameter turning on the face and various lengths of bed for between centre turning can be fitted up to 10ft. The lathe can accept various attachments such as an 8in circular saw on a rise-and-fall table, a planer, a belt sander, and a mortising table. These can convert the lathe to a universal woodworking machine of considerable power and versatility.

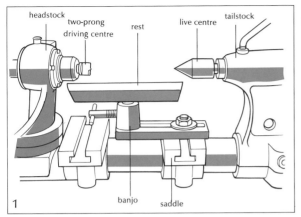

1

A standard woodturning lathe has a headstock and a tailstock. The headstock contains the means of changing speed which will vary with the diameter of the work turned. The tailstock supports the end of the work. The lathe carries a saddle, banjo and rest on which the lathe tools are placed when turning wood.

2

If you bend your right arm and place your hand on your right shoulder, then the height of the elbow above ground-level should be the height of the drive axis of the lathe between centres. If the height of the drive axis between the driving head and the tailstock is higher than your elbow, this will not be too much of a disadvantage; however, if the drive axis is too low, the user may suffer some discomfort and backache.

When working between centres, the tool rest should be between ¾in and 1in below the drive axis. This will allow the bevel on the turning tool to rub the work and the cutting edge to cut finely without losing its sharpness too quickly. The same considerations apply when working on the face, and the only occasion when a tool rest should be moved above the drive axis is when a scraping tool is used, since this tool is always used pointing down.

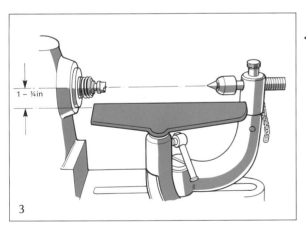

3

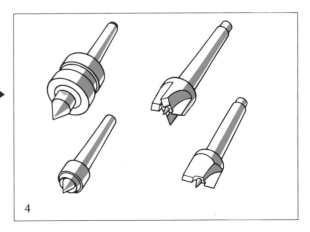

4

The tailstock can carry either a live or a dead centre. A live centre rotates with the work, on bearings, and reduces friction. A dead centre has no bearings and care should be taken that it is lubricated either with candlewax or beeswax. Driving centres can be of a two-prong, four-prong or, for certain operations, no-prong centre (ring or point centre). In practice, the two-prong drive is adequate and less expensive and, since it is easier to indent two prongs into end-grain than four, it will normally hold more securely.

Roughing gouges vary in size from ¾in to 1½in. They are used for reducing square work between centres to a cylinder, for rapid removal of waste, and for shaping between centres. They are not suitable for face work; rounding to a disc is best achieved with a bowl gouge.

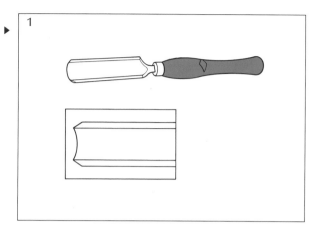

Skew chisels vary in size from ½in to 2in, the pointed end being known as the toe and the other as the heel. They are used for trimming the end of the work, making V-notches and beads, and making planing cuts with the heel leading, either on a flat surface or a taper.

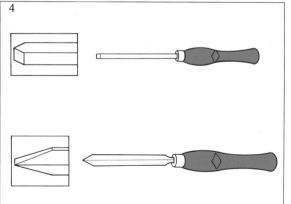

Bowl gouges are used for shaping between centres, particularly in making coves, and on the inside and outside of all bowls. The most useful size of bowl gouge is the ⅜in but gouges vary in size from a ¼in to ¾in. The ring tool is an adaptation of a much older hook tool and is used at the slowest lathe speed to hollow out material in end-grain, particularly if the wood is green.

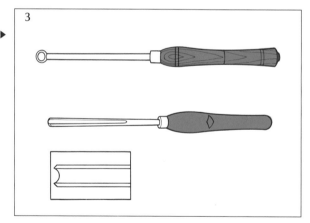

Beading tools are usually found in two sizes – ¼in and ⅜in. They are used for rounding, both between centres and in face work. They are also used in beading and with advantage in bowl work. The parting tool can be either plain, waisted or diamond shaped. It is used mainly in callipering down to diameter, can be used for rounding small beads and, of course, is used extensively for parting the wood on the lathe.

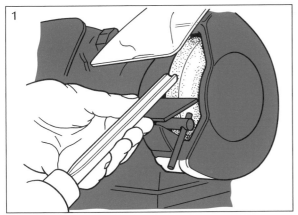

All tools are sharpened on the fine stone of the grinding wheel and then taken direct to the work. The slipstone is not used because, although its use would give a finer edge, this finer edge would be destroyed in the first few revolutions.

It is important to maintain the concave bevel which is achieved by hollow grinding on the wheel. Note that the gouge is held to give a 40 degree bevel to the cutting edge. Sharpening is complete when a thin continuous line of sparks appears along the cutting edge. The gouge is sharpened in a similar manner to sharpening a pencil. The handle is held in line with the wheel and no attempt is made to swing it from side to side. It rotates on its own axis to provide a bevel all the way around the cutting edge.

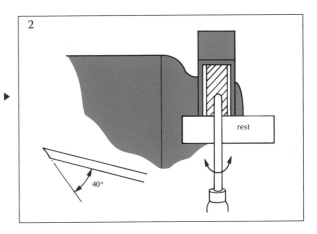

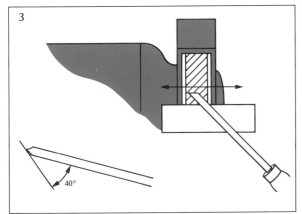

The chisel is also ground to 40 degrees and the heel is kept slightly higher than the toe to ensure that the long toe remains pointed. As with the gouge, only the weight of the tool should rest against the wheel, no attempt should be made to press the tool against the wheel; this will cause overheating and, in the case of carbon steel, softening of the metal.

The parting tool is started high up on the fine wheel and then brought down to the 40-degree position and moved from side to side until sparks appear along the cutting edge. The tool is then turned over and the process repeated. The ¼in and ⅜in beading tools are sharpened in exactly the same manner.

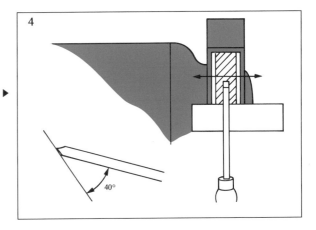

The heavy domed scraper can be used either with a normal rest or with a specially shaped rest when making finishing cuts for the inside of a bowl. The scraper is used always pointing down and with the rest as close to the work as possible. The scraper should only be used for finishing, never for shaping. Its use should be avoided if possible, since it will produce a very poor surface finish.

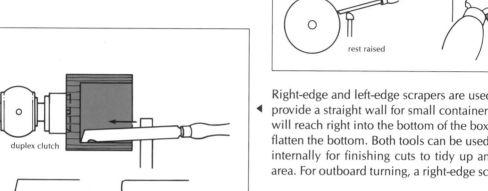

1

heavy-duty scraper rest

rest raised

Right-edge and left-edge scrapers are used as shown to provide a straight wall for small containers. These tools will reach right into the bottom of the box and will also flatten the bottom. Both tools can be used externally or internally for finishing cuts to tidy up an inaccessible area. For outboard turning, a right-edge scraper is used.

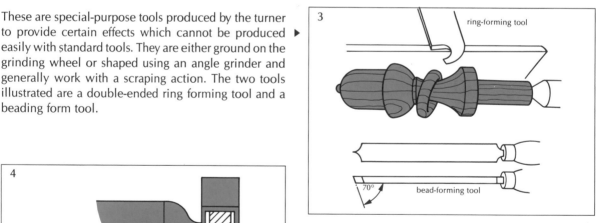

2

duplex clutch

diamond side-cutting scraper   round side-cutting scraper

These are special-purpose tools produced by the turner to provide certain effects which cannot be produced easily with standard tools. They are either ground on the grinding wheel or shaped using an angle grinder and generally work with a scraping action. The two tools illustrated are a double-ended ring forming tool and a beading form tool.

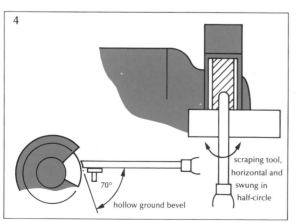

3

ring-forming tool

70° bead-forming tool

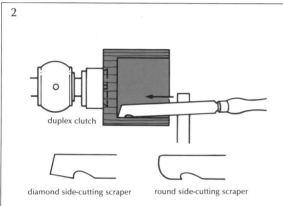

4

70°

hollow ground bevel

scraping tool, horizontal and swung in half-circle

Scraping tools are sharpened to a more oblique angle of 70 degrees in order that the cutting edge is well supported for the increased stress and wear it has to undergo. Scrapers are sharpened using the coarse stone. The scraping action removes the cutting edge more quickly than on normal turning tools. For this reason, high-speed steel scrapers, which need sharpening less often will be found valuable. Sharpening is complete when sparks appear along the cutting edge.

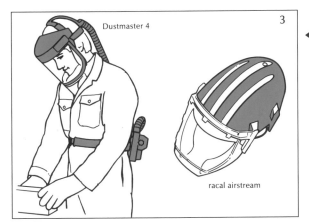

disposable moulded paper mask 1

Martindale protective mask with replaceable liner

Dust is a serious hazard, particularly if exotic timbers are being worked. A list of wood with hazard ratings is given in Appendix 1, Page 124. While not providing complete protection, the use-once-and-throw-away paper mask illustrated is useful for short-term exposure. Rubber face masks with disposable filters are more efficient.

In the normal course of events, there is no need to wear eye protection whilst working, either between centres or on the face of the lathe. Occasionally, it may be necessary to wear a lightweight visor for the sake of comfort, such as when shavings from a bowl are coming off sufficiently fast to make the turner uncomfortable. Visors have an adjustable nut at the back. They provide limited protection from shavings and no protection from dust.

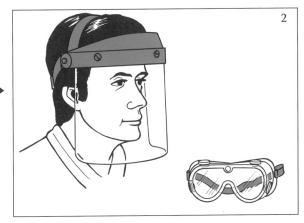

2

Some helmets fitted with portable power supplies provide filtered air over the wearer's face, and offer complete protection from dust from home-grown or imported woods. These helmets also protect the turner from flying shavings, and the flow of air avoids spectacle wearers' lenses fogging over. The equipment is provided with rechargeable batteries and is neither heavy nor cumbersome.

Dustmaster 4 3

racal airstream

Specially designed woodturning jackets with a high collar and buttoned sleeves, provide comfortable and practical dress. The simple dust jacket is adequate for most purposes, provided a well-tucked-in neck scarf is worn as protection from shavings. The carpenter's apron is not satisfactory since the front pocket fills with shavings very quickly. As a general rule, there should be no loose clothing to catch in the moving parts of the lathe.

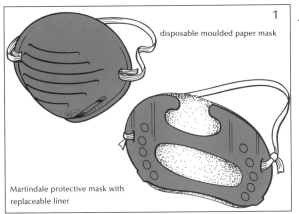

4

Once the wood has been mounted between the driving and tail centres and the rest is in position, the work must be rotated by hand before switching on. The rest should be as close to the work as possible and parallel to it. Rotating the wood in this manner avoids the work striking the rest, upsetting the driving centre location and damaging the material.

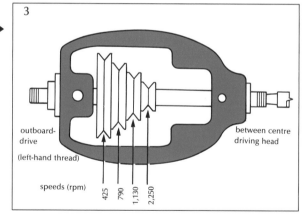

If the rest is not completely firm, the lathe is not safe for use. Check the firmness of the rest by tugging at one or other end before switching on. If there is the slightest movement, check the firmness of all rests, clamps and nuts.

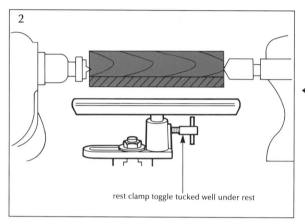

rest clamp toggle tucked well under rest

The correct speed must be selected before switching on. As a rule of thumb, if the work is 2in or less in diameter, then a speed of approximately 2,000 r.p.m. will be suitable. The greater the dimensions of the work, the slower the speed required for turning. For example, a ⅜in-diameter lace bobbin will require a much higher speed for working than a 6in-diameter skittle. A full range of wood sizes and speeds is given in Appendix 2, page 124.

3

outboard-drive

(left-hand thread)

between centre driving head

speeds (rpm) 425 790 1,130 2,250

Check that the tailstock is properly secure and wound in sufficiently to engrave the two driving points of the driving head. If the tailstock is of the dead-centre variety it must be lubricated with candlewax or beeswax. If the tailstock is not secure when the lathe is running, an increasingly loud clattering will be heard. The lathe should be stopped immediately and the source of the noise found and corrected.

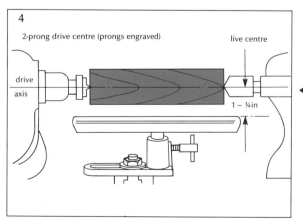

2-prong drive centre (prongs engraved)

live centre

drive axis

1 – ¾in

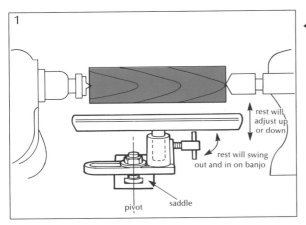

To avoid trapping your hand between the revolving work and the rest, the rest should be removed for sanding or polishing; allowing the hand to move under the work so that if either abrasive paper or polishing materials catch in the wood, they are thrown forward and away from the operator.

Until you have experience on the lathe, it is advisable to adjust the rest for angle and height, etc. only with the lathe stationary. With experience you will find that you can safely adjust the rest with the work running and, indeed, most woodturners do this. If a mistake is made and the work touches the rest while the lathe is running, you risk damaging perhaps an hour's intricate work.

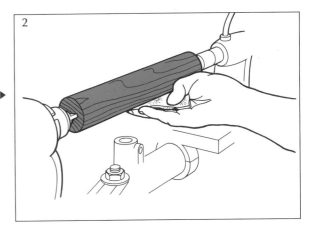

A vibrating lathe does not allow good woodturning and the main cause of vibration on a woodturning lathe is unbalanced material. Careful use of the band-saw or hand-saw should prevent out-of-balance vibration but, should it occur, then the speed will have to be reduced until the vibration is minimized. Vibration can be reduced by weighting the lathe bed (e.g. with concrete blocks underneath), by bolting back to a wall, or by placing sheet rubber under the legs.

Keep the lathe uncluttered by re-racking tools not immediately wanted for the job in hand. A convenient way of racking tools is the saddle-bucket style where the tools are stored blade-down and are all readily to hand. To help select the tool you want, it is a good idea to number sequentially the tools on the handle end. A suggested numbering sequence is given in Appendix 3, page 124.

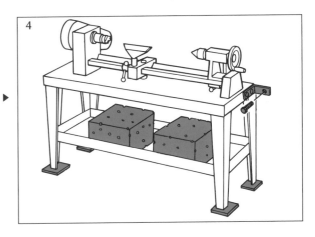

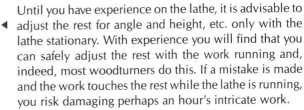

Two different methods of finding centres are shown here. Crossed diagonals will give a centre but normally require the wood to be held in a vice and the use of a straight edge. The squared-in system means that by using the traditional carpenter's-pencil–and-middle-finger technique, a reduced square can be drawn on the end, in which the eye can readily find a centre with the bradawl. This can be done without leaving the lathe or needing a straight edge.

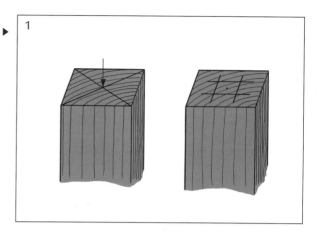

If a large number of similar items are being turned, then it is useful to construct a small jig of the type shown here where centre is found easily and with consistent accuracy by tapping the work onto a sharpened point. Such a method would be used for the production of miniature bannisters for dolls' houses, required in multiples of six or seven dozen.

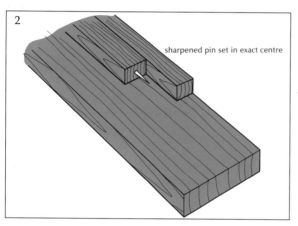

sharpened pin set in exact centre

The choice between a two-prong or a four-prong driving centre can be resolved by asking which is the easier to drive into end-grain. The two-prong drive penetrates more deeply and, thus, holds more firmly. If you already have a four-prong drive, it can be improved by removing two of its prongs. In the case of a very hard wood, it would be impossible to mark centres with a bradawl or engrave a two-prong driving head, and it is necessary to make a saw-cut either with a band-saw or tenon-saw to provide a reliable drive.

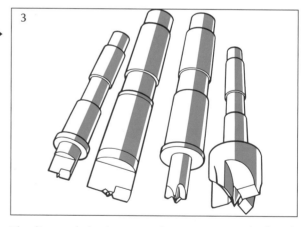

The live and dead centres shown are typical of such centres provided by all lathe manufacturers. The live centre is always larger in diameter to accommodate robust bearings. The dead centre has no moving parts. The dead centre should be lubricated either with candlewax or beeswax before use. Ideally, only a live tail centre should be used, as it means one less thing for the lathe operator to worry about.

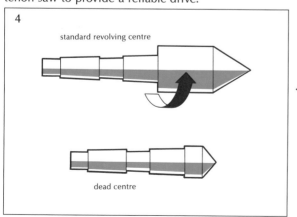

standard revolving centre

dead centre

◄ A small hole is made with the bradawl in both ends of the work, where the centres have been found. A spare driving centre, kept on the lathe bench with a mallet, is useful in indenting the wood prior to mounting, provided that it is of exactly the same pattern as the one mounted in the headstock.

The material is mounted into the driving head first, and into the tailstock second. The tailstock is wound in ► tightly and then backed off by a half-turn to reduce the pressure on the bearings. The tool rest is set close to the work, ¾in below the centre of the drive axis, parallel with the work, and checked for firmness.

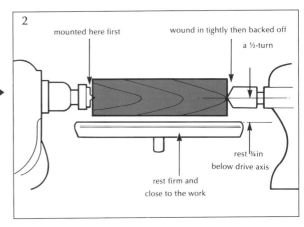

The correct speed is checked for the size of work ◄ between centres. As a rough guide, if the work is 2in or less in diameter, a speed of approximately 2,000r.p.m. will be satisfactory. For turning small-diameter work, such as lace bobbins or ball-pen sleeves, the lathe should run at maximum speed. For bowls of 20–24in diameter, the minimum speed will be required.

Setting the speed of the lathe to run too slowly will not improve safety, but will induce boredom and produce a ► poor finish on the work. In the case of a speed being chosen too high, there will be excessive noise and the shavings will come from the work fast enough to sting the hands of the operator. The condition is not unsafe, but it is not comfortable and the speed should be corrected.

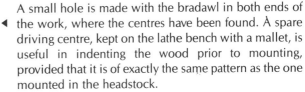

Lathe Speed Check Card

Too High	Too Low
1. Noise	1. No noise from the lathe, but loud knocking from the wood.
2. Vibration	2. Surface finish is torn and rough.
3. Shavings coming off fast enough to sting the turner's hands.	3. Very slow to obtain any results.

First Rule (steps 1–4) Always turn from high to low. 'High' is defined as being nearest to the rest, and 'Low' as being farthest from the rest. The illustration shows a roughing gouge turning a taper from high to low between centres. The reason behind this rule is that the turner must always cut 'with the grain'. Cutting from low to high, against the rule, results in a rough finish and torn edges.

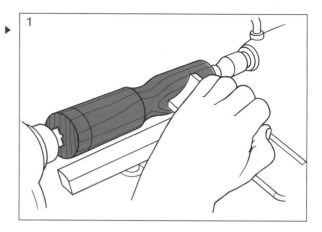

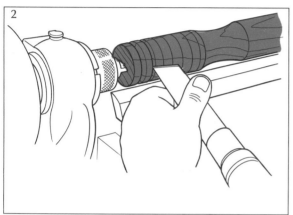

In turning a V-notch, the first movement is for the skew chisel to make a small nick on the pencilled mark. The second and third movements are illustrated turning from high to low, alternately from side to side, to increase the depth and width of the V-notch. This method gives complete control of both the shape and the depth of the V-notch. Full details of cutting the notches can be found on page 21.

The beads are cut with a ⅜in beading tool, again turning from high to low on either side of the bead. The tool is rolled downwards from high to low. Full details of forming beads can be found on page 22. The beading tool can be used in a number of ways in addition to forming beads, notably for finishing cuts on the bases and outside curve of bowls.

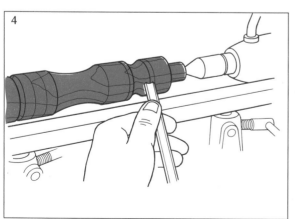

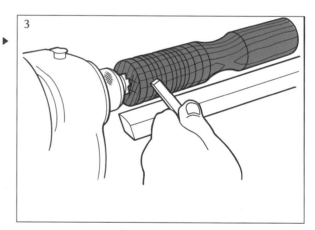

In forming a cove, the bowl gouge travels from high to low, pausing at the bottom of the cove. The gouge is re-positioned on the opposite shoulder of the cove and then travels down, again from high to low. Full details of two alternative methods of forming coves are given on page 23. Both methods follow the first rule of woodturning. One permits the quick cutting of deep coves, the other a fairly safe cut for single-handed working with callipers.

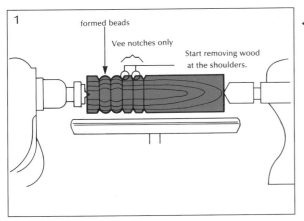

Second rule (steps 5–8)   Start by taking off from where the maximum material must come. In the case of forming a bead, this will be the two shoulders, and the beading tool is used on either shoulder alternately with the bevel rubbing, cutting from high to low. The bead will start to form in its final shape as the shoulders are removed.

Applying this rule to turning a cove, the gouge is used to make a small furrow in the centre of the cove and then to swing from left and right, down to centre, turning from high to low and taking off where the maximum material must come from until the cove is completed.

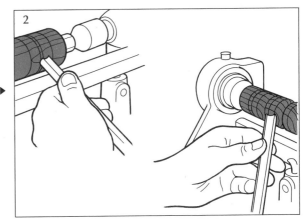

In forming a taper, start taking off where the minimum diameter of the taper will finally be. The illustration shows the sequence of cuts made to produce an even taper.

If the rule of starting to take off where the maximum must come from is not followed, certain definite effects will be seen in making beads, coves and tapers, and these are illustrated here. You can see where the woodturner has started taking off at the wrong point.

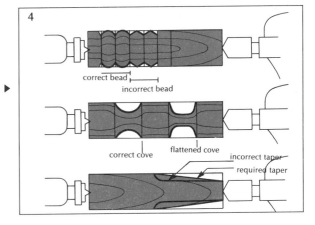

With safety checks complete, switch on and check for any faults. Undue noise could be due to any of the following: excess speed, loose tailstock, work brushing the rest, drive belt incorrectly tensioned. The lathe should be steady, free from vibration and relatively silent. If vibration is found, the work may be out of balance, the tailstock may not be tightened, the motor speed may be too high or there could be a loose fitting on the lathe.

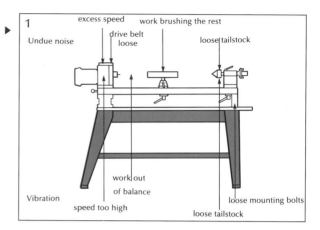

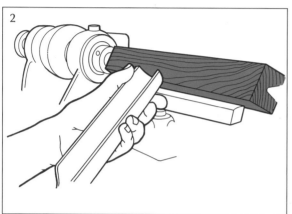

The tool is held at the angle shown so that the bevel rubs the wood with the cutting edge just cutting the squared work. There is no necessity to plane off the four square edges. This angle allows the turner to see clearly what is happening at the cutting edge and also ensures maximum life of the cutting edge through a cutting rather than a scraping action. The guiding hand must hold the tool blade, and also rub along the rest.

As work progresses in roughing down the material, the roughing gouge can be used running from either right or left, or it can be used to 'spot treat' any point that looks high. It is not necessary to stop the lathe to examine whether the work is round; any flats which still remain can be easily detected by running the fingers of the left hand over the work.

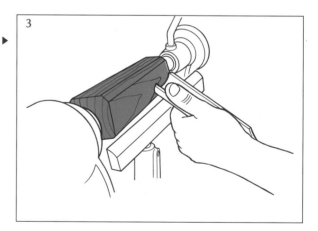

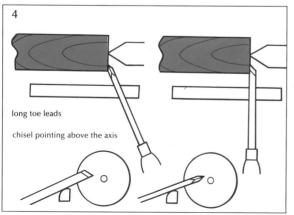

When the work comes from the band-saw or hand-saw, the ends are seldom square. The tailstock end can be squared in the manner shown, with a skew chisel. Beginners may find the alternative method of squaring shown on the right a little easier but it will not produce quite such a clean finish. Note that in both these skew chisel cuts the toe is pointing up above the centre of the drive axis.

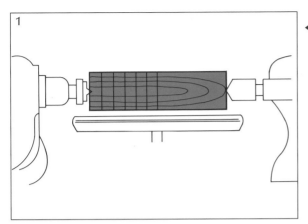

Having reduced the work to a smooth cylinder, the V-notches are set out with a pencil and a section of tape-measure with the work revolving. All setting-out operations, whether between centres or on face work, are done with the work revolving.

The first cut is made with the toe of a skew chisel, the heel uppermost. It is a stroke that goes into the work directly at right angles to the cylinder, on the pencil line, to produce an initial shallow nick. The cut should be quick and the tool should not be allowed to rest in the work longer than a fraction of a second. Should it rest longer than this, the tool will be unnecessarily blunted.

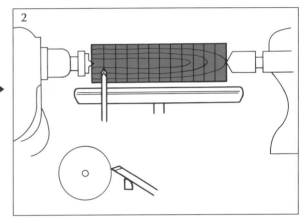

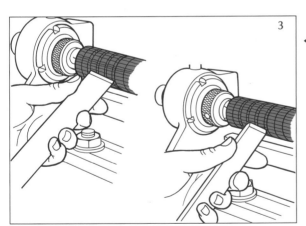

For the second cut, remove the skew chisel from the work and re-position it at 45 degrees to the left. Then roll it up to vertical while pushing into the initial nick. The tool is then removed from the work again, placed at 45 degrees to the right of the nick and then the operation is repeated rolling up to vertical. In both cases only the point of the chisel does the cutting. These second and third cuts are repeated until the notch is of the depth and shape required.

The turner should complete the remaining V-notches without striving to make them identical, because the final operation will be to view all the notches made, and bring them all to an exact copy by adjusting where necessary. There should be no feathering left in the centre of the notch and if the point has been used correctly in cutting the sides, there should be no feathering on the surface of the cylinder either.

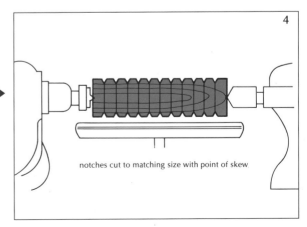

notches cut to matching size with point of skew

The V-notches having been completed on the cylinder, they can be converted to beads by the use of a ⅜in beading tool. The tool is used at right angles to the work and cuts from high to low. It makes cuts from the shoulders of the bead in order to start where the maximum must be removed. ▶

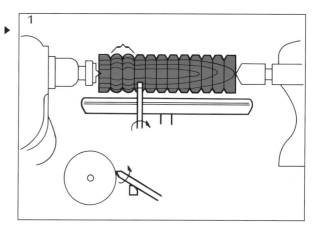

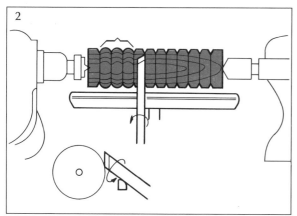

◀ Beads can be formed with the heel of the skew, with a parting tool, or with a square chisel. In each case the cuts must be made from high to low and commence where the maximum material is to be removed to form the beads. In each of these cases, the tool is used at right angles to the work and is rotated over and down to form the bead.

Should a long length of beading be required, for example to be used for antique restoration, then it may ▶ be necessary to make a small form tool which can accurately reproduce each bead profile with the minimum of effort. The tool acts as a scraping tool and is, therefore, shown pointing down. The rest is above the drive axis. The tool is made by grinding on the coarse wheel. When the beading is complete, it is sawn to two identical strips.

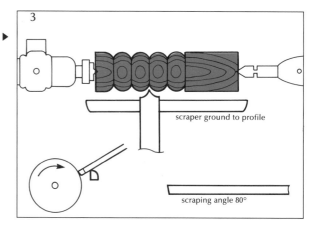

scraper ground to profile

scraping angle 80°

◀ The illustration shows a Dale Nish beading tool in use for bead forming. As in the previous case, this form of tool utilizes a scraping action and the tool is used pointing downwards from a raised rest.

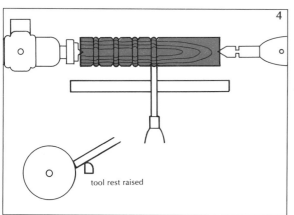

tool rest raised

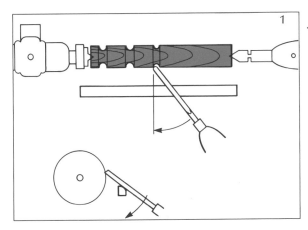

The first method, described here, is the 'fail safe' system with a bowl gouge moving through 90 degrees in order to make the cut, starting in the centre to follow the rule that the turner should start where the maximum material is to be removed. The tool handle is low down and the bevel is rubbing. The illustration shows the cut from the left to the bottom of the cove.

The illustration shows the cut from the right side to the bottom of the cove; again the tool handle is low and the bevel rubbing. In both these cuts the tool must approach the work at right angles and then swing down to the bottom of the cove. It must stop at this point and come down on the other side of the cove since if it were to continue up the other side, it would produce a poor finish.

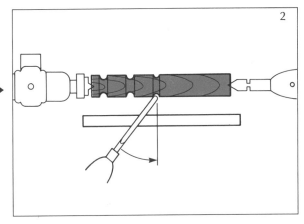

The second method depends upon the bowl gouge being angled over on its side. It enters the work at right angles, with the bevel rubbing, and is held very firmly until the initial cut into the wood is completed, and the bevel has a shoulder to rub against. At the end of the stroke in the centre of the cove the bowl gouge will be upright.

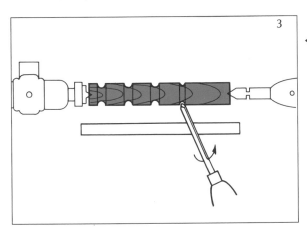

This illustration shows the second method where the cut from the right-hand side of the cove is executed with the tool on its side and firmly held until there is sufficient material for the bevel to rub; again the gouge becomes upright at the bottom of the cove. This cut will produce a good finish, but there is a chance of the gouge slipping on entry if not held firmly.

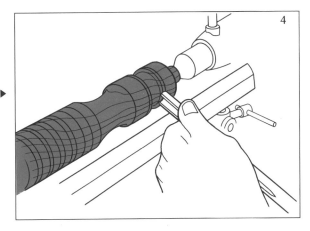

Pummels occur very often in bannisters, table legs and chair legs. The most usual form is a convex pummel, as illustrated, and this is formed with a skew chisel applied directly onto the square wood. A V-notch is cut as shown on page 21, and the waste removed with a roughing gouge and beading tool. This V-notch is progressively deepened and widened to the required depth, and to the marked pummel line. ▶

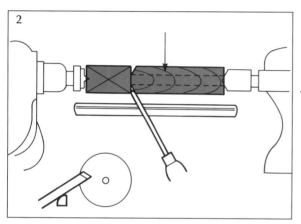

1

waste removed with beading tool

waste removed with roughing gouge

pummel formed with toe of skew chisel

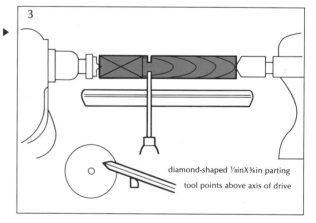

2

◀ A skew chisel is used to form a square pummel, the angle of the chisel being the same as that illustrated in step 4, page 20. For a standard staircase bannister, a number of such cuts will have to be made, with the waste carefully removed.

An alternative way of forming a square pummel is to use a parting tool to come down to the required depth, leaving a small amount of waste which is then cleared with a skew chisel in the way shown in step 2 above. Waste is progressively removed with the roughing gouge or beading tool until the required depth is reached. ▶

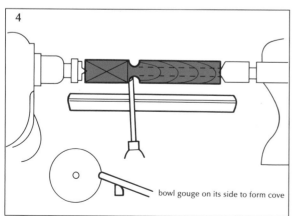

3

diamond-shaped ⅛in X ¾in parting tool points above axis of drive

4

bowl gouge on its side to form cove

◀ Very occasionally, a concave pummel has to be made and it is formed using a bowl gouge. A cove is turned, by either of the two methods, onto the square work, and the waste is removed using a roughing gouge and beading tool. The size of the bowl gouge in use is generally determined by the size of the work. For most purposes, a ⅜in gouge is adequate.

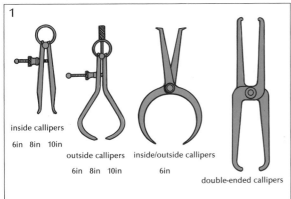

1

inside callipers

6in 8in 10in

outside callipers   inside/outside callipers

6in 8in 10in   6in

double-ended callipers

The illustration shows, from left to right, internal, external and thickness registering callipers. In practice the internal callipers are rarely used. Fingers used to judge the thickness of bowls are generally quicker and more accurate. The external callipers are used extensively, particularly in copy turning.

The gauge bars shown in the illustrations run (1) ½in to 1¼in and (2) from ⅜in to 1⅛in. The gauges are used in the same manner as external callipers but have the added advantage that they burnish the wood at the required diameter when they pass through. They are of particular use in fitting chair legs to seats, etc. They cannot lose their measured distance as callipers can sometimes do when the knurled nut is allowed to vibrate or if they are knocked.

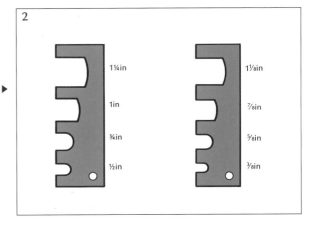

2

1¼in

1in

¾in

½in

1⅛in

⅞in

⅝in

⅜in

When making croquet balls or skittle balls, etc., a sighting disc is used for final shaping of the work together with external callipers. The pin gauge shown is used for repetition work such as lace bobbin production.

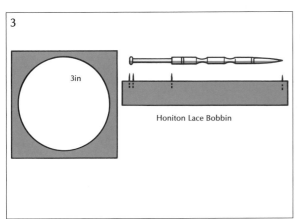

3

3in

Honiton Lace Bobbin

For copy turning, a pattern stick is used with lettered gauges which have the knurled nut taped over. This prevents it moving and changing its dimension and also provides a place for convenient lettering. Copy turning is dealt with in detail on page 85. Profiles or templates are not used, simply the pattern stick and a set of callipers to work from a given example.

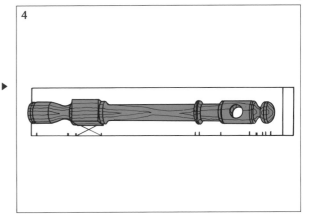

4

The illustration shows a finished bradawl handle incorporating a brass ferrule and a sharpened nail. The ferrule can be cut from offcuts of copper piping available from your local plumber, or can be obtained from tool manufacturers in brass if required. The material used for the handle can be any attractive hardwood – ash, elm, beech or boxwood would be ideal. Rough down the blank to a cylinder and square the end at the tailstock. Set out the bradawl dimensions as shown.

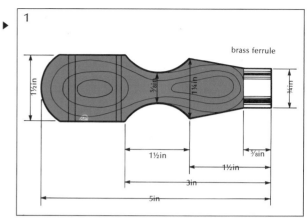

Hold a diamond-shaped parting tool in the right hand with the index finger on the metal and the palm on the wooden handle. Hold the callipers in the left hand with the fingers round the knurled nut to prevent it moving. Calliper down on the ferrule diameter as shown until the calliper passes through from front to back; no pressure is required. Repeat this cut at the other end of the ferrule marking. Remove the waste with any convenient gouge.

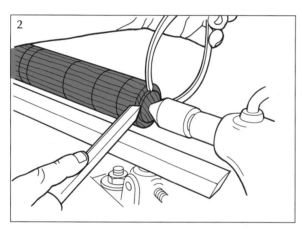

Test the ferrule for fit. It should eventually be an interference fit that can be wound on using a vice. Take off material gradually using a ⅜in beading tool until the required fit is achieved. The finishing cuts with the ⅜in beading tool to fit the ferrule should be carried out in the following way. Treat the beading tool as a square chisel and produce a planing cut, as shown, with the bevel rubbing along the work. This produces a fine finish and also allows fine removal of material for this operation.

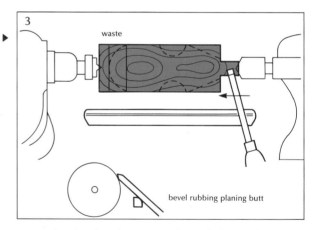

Using the ⅜in bowl gouge in the right hand (forefinger on the metal and palm on the wooden handle), and the callipers in the left hand (as before, holding the knurled nut), complete the waist in the bradawl handle as though you were making a cove, as on page 23.

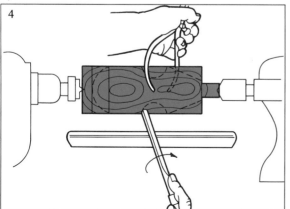

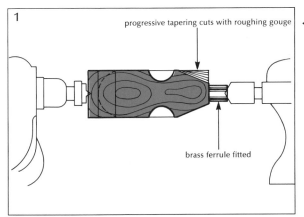

progressive tapering cuts with roughing gouge

brass ferrule fitted

The taper between the ferrule and the cove is formed using a 1½in roughing gouge. This follows the rule that turners should use the largest tool possible for each operation. A similar rule applies to painting, where the largest brush possible is used for the same reasons – to save time and improve the finish.

The tool handle is rounded at the back, using the toe of a skew chisel to cut an increasing depth of V-notch as each cut is made. Leaving about ¼in of diameter in place, sanding sealer (cellulose based) is applied, using a rag or brush, with the work stationary.

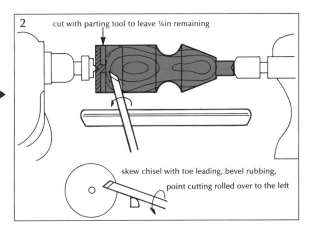

cut with parting tool to leave ¼in remaining

skew chisel with toe leading, bevel rubbing, point cutting rolled over to the left

When dry, (usually after about four minutes), the work is run on the lathe and given five seconds smoothing with grade 0000 wire wool. It is then burnished with shavings, keeping the hand moving so that the hand and the work are not overheated in any one place, causing burning. This will produce a hard shine and bring out the best figure in the work without making the tool handle slippery in use as a wax finish would.

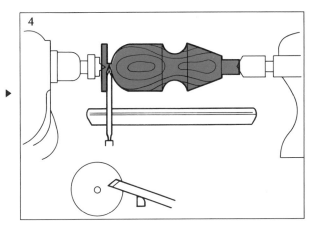

rest removed

hand and shavings in constant motion for 4–5 seconds

Part off the bradawl handle using a skew chisel in increasing V-notch cuts with the left hand over the lathe supporting the work when it is parted through. You could part off with a parting tool or a junior hack-saw, or the work could be taken off the lathe and parted on the band-saw.

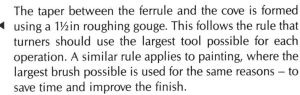

A Jacob's chuck can be mounted in the headstock or the tailstock. The No. 1 morse taper can be sleeved to fit No. 2 or No. 3 morse taper headstocks and tailstocks. Here is a three-jaw chuck which will accept twist drills, saw-tooth bits and flat bits. Morse taper twist bits are available generally in No. 1 MT which will fit into either the head or tail and can be sleeved for No. 2 or No. 3 MT.

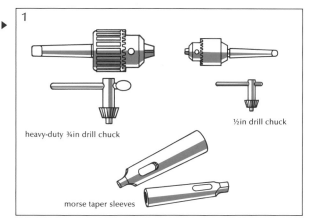

1

heavy-duty ¾in drill chuck

½in drill chuck

morse taper sleeves

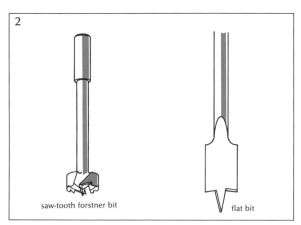

2

saw-tooth forstner bit

flat bit

The saw-tooth bits illustrated on the left provide a very smooth cut finish and, once they have entered the work, the parallel sides hold the direction of drilling steady. Flat bits, as shown on the right, can be used when drilling on the lathe. They are cheaper than saw-tooth bits, but do not give the same finish and are prone to wander.

The choice of whether the Jacob's chuck is mounted in the head or the tail is entirely a matter of personal preference or convenience of handling. For example, in boring the long hole for a pepper mill it is more convenient to use a tail-mounted Jacob's chuck stationary, and let the work revolve from the headstock held in a combination, or duplex, chuck.

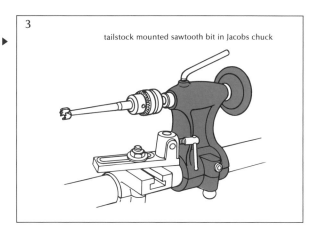

3

tailstock mounted sawtooth bit in Jacobs chuck

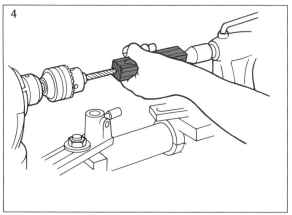

4

An example of where a head mounting of the Jacob's chuck would be convenient is in the use of a twist bit to drill for the knife tang in a knife handle blank. Note that the handle is drilled while still in the square; this is to allow for the possibility that the drill bit may move slightly off-centre. All drilling on the lathe should be completed at the slowest rate of which the lathe is capable.

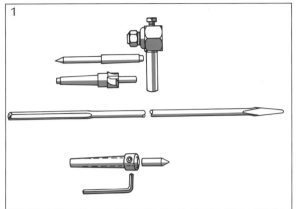

The $\frac{5}{16}$ in auger, counterbore and hollow centre are illustrated. An alternative pattern of equipment is available in $\frac{3}{8}$ in. The $\frac{5}{16}$ in drill hole will accept the EC standard three-core cable. The material is bored in the square in order to correct any tendency for the auger to move off-centre.

The hollow tail centre is effectively a dead centre and must be lubricated with candlewax or beeswax. The auger is fed in through the tailstock and hollow tail centre, keeping the handle slightly above the axis, and with the trough of the auger upright. The auger will cut if the trough is upside-down, but when withdrawing the auger all the dust will discharge in the barrel of the tailstock and clog it.

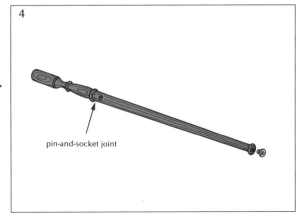

this distance determines
the thickness of cut

hollow tail centre

cutting edge

close-up of auger head

As before, the slowest speed is used to avoid overheating and the auger is fed into the material not more than 1in for each cut. Note the masking tape marker on the auger to avoid inadvertently pushing the auger into the driving head. Feed in 1in at each stroke, removing debris each time.

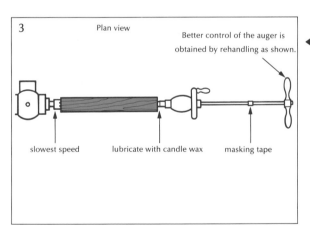

Plan view

Better control of the auger is obtained by rehandling as shown.

slowest speed   lubricate with candle wax   masking tape

The work is drilled in both directions using the auger, and quite long lengths can be bored. However, there is usually a need for a pin-and-socket joint to connect lengths of the work when a standard lamp is constructed. At the top of the standard, a threaded brass nipple is screwed into the $\frac{5}{16}$ in hole to accept a light fitting.

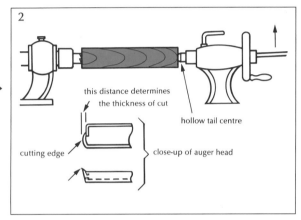

pin-and-socket joint

These cuts aim to provide a finished surface which needs the minimum of sanding, if any. A planing cut ▶ with a skew chisel is illustrated with the heel leading and the toe, the trailing point, kept high and well away from the work. Note that only the bottom half of the skew chisel is actually cutting. The rest height in all of thee finishing cuts is normal, that is to say ¾–1in below the drive axis.

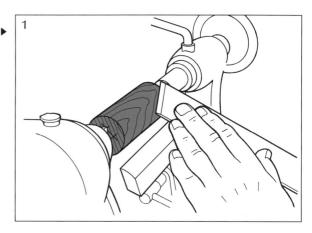

This rounding cut with the heel of the skew chisel can ◀ be considered a finishing cut since it gives a fine burnished finish, from the bevel rubbing the work as it rotates. All finishing cuts should be made with the tool freshly sharpened. The aim is to remove the minimum amount of wood to show a fine finish, without altering the shape of the work. Remember that if you suspect a tool is going blunt, you are almost certainly correct.

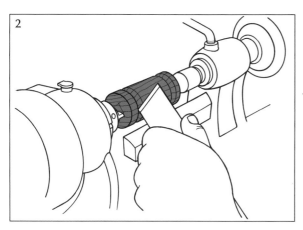

A ⅜in beading tool can be used to give a facing cut in a similar manner to a square chisel. The illustration ▶ shows a beading tool giving a facing cut on the base of a bowl recess. The leading point is picking up the material and shearing to the edge of the recess.

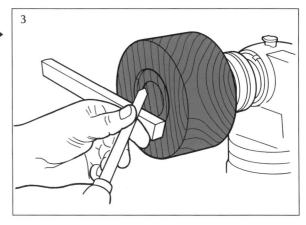

A planing cut with a ⅜in beading tool, in this case ◀ acting as a square chisel, with the bevel rubbing and burnishing the work. This tool works to best advantage when making 'spot treatment' cuts on previous tool marks, as opposed to the long, flowing cut of the bowl gouge used for finishing. Move the tool, the tool rest and yourself around the outside of the bowl so that you are working always at right angles to the face, with the handle well down and bevel rubbing.

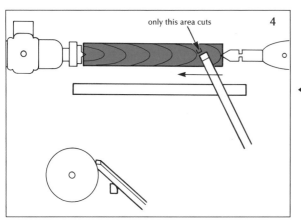

only this area cuts

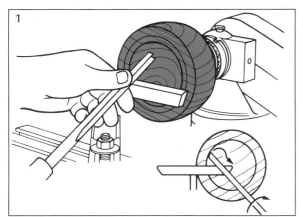

Using a ⅜in bowl gouge inside a bowl to produce a finishing cut is best done by using a shearing cut following the path shown in the illustration. It will be necessary for the turner to take one or two paces backwards in order to allow this cut to lie correctly inside the bowl. The bevel rubs and the tool is over on its side.

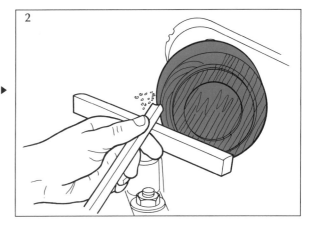

The outside profile of the bowl can also be given a finishing shearing cut with the bowl gouge. The bevel must be kept rubbing all the time, which means that the angle of the gouge to the bowl must be changed constantly as the tool rounds the outside of the work. Notice that when working on the inside of the bowl one works to the inside, and when working on the outside one works to the outside.

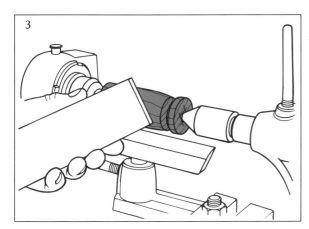

The planing cut with the square chisel is similar to that illustrated in step 1, page 30 showing the planing cut with the skew chisel. With the square chisel, there is the advantage that the blade can be reversed if it is starting to lose its cutting edge.

The large roughing gouge (1½in) is capable of good finishing cuts, either on cylinders or tapers, provided that the tool is freshly sharpened, is used in a smooth and light manner, and follows the rule of cutting from high to low.

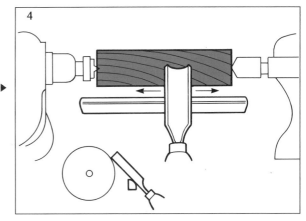

The wooden screw box and metal tap are traditional tools for cutting wood screw threads. A different size box and tap must be used for each size of wood screw thread. The box has a V-cutter which can be removed for sharpening; the tap is used with a simple wrench of the pattern used in metal screw tapping.

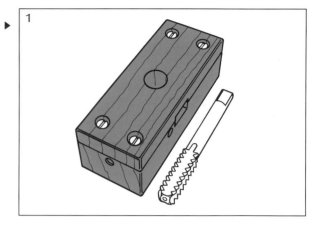

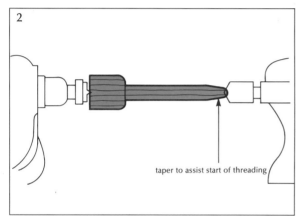

Frequently a wood screw will require a squared section, and the illustration shows a prepared blank with squared end, convex pummel, turned dowel, and taper. The turned dowel is given a coating of candlewax to assist in the screw threading operation and placed upright in a vice.

The screw box is turned onto the dowel and pressed downwards until its threading catches and pulls the cutter down the dowel for the rest of the threaded distance. The box is not turned back at any point as in metal screw cutting, but continues in one movement to the bottom of the required screw thread. It is then unwound and taken off.

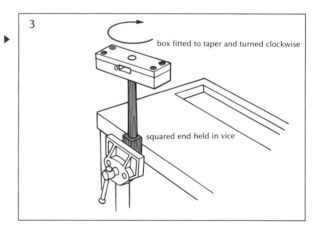

The material for the threaded nut is drilled and tapped whilst in the square and finally shaped between centres on the lathe. A table of drilled hole sizes for various sizes of screw thread is given in Appendix 4, page 125.

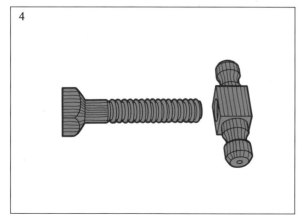

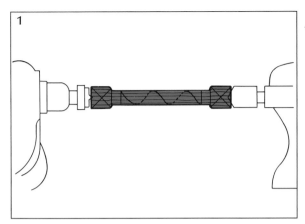

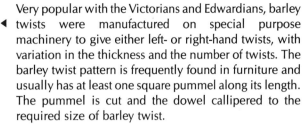

Very popular with the Victorians and Edwardians, barley twists were manufactured on special purpose machinery to give either left- or right-hand twists, with variation in the thickness and the number of twists. The barley twist pattern is frequently found in furniture and usually has at least one square pummel along its length. The pummel is cut and the dowel callipered to the required size of barley twist.

The lower diameter of the barley twist is set out in a sinusoidal curve to the required pitch and distance. An indexing attachment to the lathe is useful in this operation. Masking tape laid on the work in a spiral will be found useful here. One edge of the tape will be used as the final guide-line when the tape is secured in the required spiral.

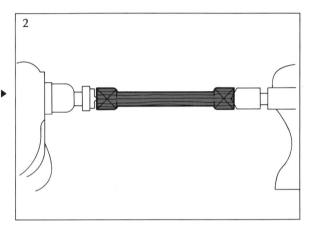

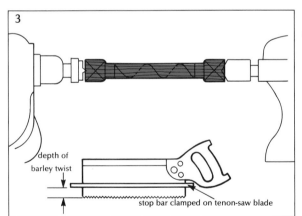

depth of
barley twist

stop bar clamped on tenon-saw blade

A stop is placed on a tenon-saw to give the required depth of the barley twist hollow and then the saw-cut is made along the line set out in step 2 above. The indexing attachment mentioned above is ideal for steadying the work during this operation. However, if this is not available, clamping the squared section of the work to the lathe bar by two offcuts of wood on either side, and clamps above and below, are adequate.

Using the depth line as a guide, the barley twist is cut with a shaping tool (a Surform round rasp) and finally sanded to finish. This is a time-consuming operation, and if a number of barley twist articles are required, consideration should be given to production on an automatic lathe. A router with a suitable bit mounted above the lathe and free to move along the work is a possible solution. Almost certainly, a second pair of hands will be required to turn the work by hand as the router advances.

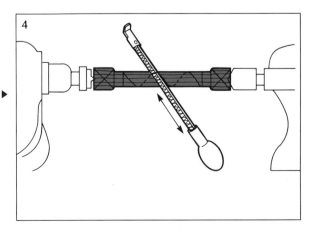

The faceplates illustrated are, from the left, the Coronet Major, the Startrite Graduate, and the Myford ML8. Faceplates normally have four holes for screw mounting, but in practice only two need ever be used. In use, the screws are driven into the work, the work is turned, and when the screws are removed the holes will have to be filled. It is possible to avoid these screw holes if the part of the work containing the screw holes is considered as waste, or some method of adhesive as in steps 2 and 3 below is used.

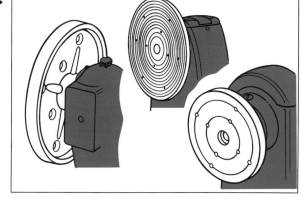

Double-sided carpet tape, can be used to mount bowl blanks onto the wooden discs mounted on a faceplate. It is essential that both surfaces be flat and free from dust, and that when the parts are taped together they are clamped for three to four minutes. The most convenient method of clamping is to use the tailstock and headstock of the lathe. This method allows single-chucking production of bowls without screw holes in the base.

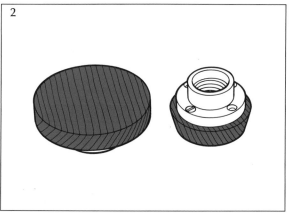

Hot-melt glue from an electric glue gun will hold the bowl blank to the wooden disc on a faceplate, and also allow single-chucked bowls to be produced without screw holes in the base. Alternatively, both methods can be used to mount the bowl blank as an initial operation before using a combination or duplex chuck to hollow out the centre of the bowl.

3

Work Mounting Summary

Single chucking	Double chucking
1. Two screws-faceplate to work	First operation as in single chucking
2. Double-sided tape	Then,
3. Hot-melt glue	1. Jacob's chuck
4. Screw chuck	2. Duplex chuck
5. Pin chuck	3. Combination chuck
6. Cup chuck	(a) Expanding collet
	(b) Gripping collet
	(c) Split-ring mounting

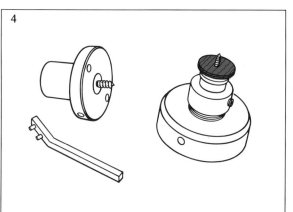

Coronet Major (left) and Startrite Graduate (right) screw chucks are shown. These provide a quick and versatile means of holding material, but they do not hold well in end-grain. They are ideal for small finial and knob production.

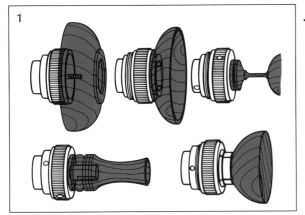

The Craft Supplies combination chuck and the expanding collet chuck for the Startrite Graduate and Coronet Major are shown. They are most frequently used as expanding collet chucks into pre-formed recesses in the bases of bowl blanks. They give a very firm fixing and different sizes of collet give variety to accommodate all sizes of face work.

The Myford cup chuck is shown here. This is a simple and quite robust method of holding the wood. Once fitted, the work must not be moved from the chuck until the article is complete. This chuck will also accept a triple compression collet and screw chuck. When used with the compression collets, work can be safely held whilst projecting up to 8in from the chuck.

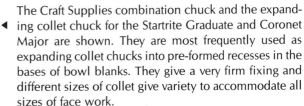

Split-ring chucks provide a very firm means of holding work in end-grain. Shown here are the Startrite Graduate and Coronet Major split-ring chucks. The mounting they provide offers a means of holding a cantilevered piece of work to 10in from the headstock, for example long-stemmed vases or goblets.

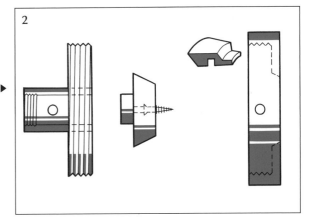

split rings

prepared work

Multi-purpose chucks also provide the facility of ring chucks and screw chucks. The pattern shown is the 6-in-1 Universal Chuck by Hattersley and Davidson Ltd, which can be used as an expanding collet chuck, a split-ring chuck, and internal screw chuck and a faceplate, as well as in the roles illustrated. The work size is limited to the internal diameter of the ring.

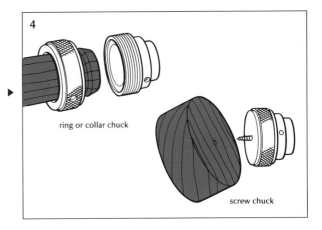

ring or collar chuck

screw chuck

Multistar (steps 1–4) This sectioned drawing of the Colchester Multistar chuck illustrates its operation and major components. It has the ability not only to expand its jaws into a recess, but also to contract them to grip a spigot.

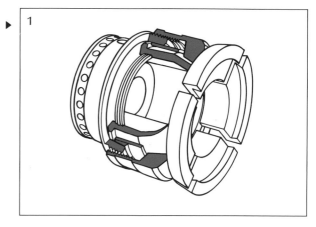

The range of sizes of jaw for this chuck is illustrated, together with pin chucks and screw chucks. The pin chucks and the larger screw chucks can be used on an unprepared face, for example a bark face, eliminating the need for preliminary planing. Bark-edged bowls are also produced by this method.

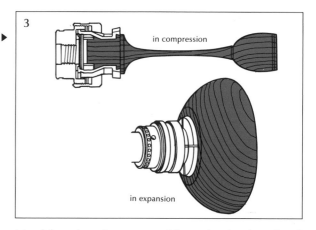

Illustrations of holding in expansion and in compression are given here to demonstrate this piece of equipment's versatility. Along with all duplex chucks, it has the advantage of being able to remove and replace the work at any time during the turning operation without loss of concentricity.

in compression

in expansion

Metal faceplate rings are useful to schools where bowl blanks have to be dismounted weekly and left until the instruction resumes. The metal-to-metal contact between the faceplate ring and the expanding jaws ensures that the blank centres accurately on each occasion.

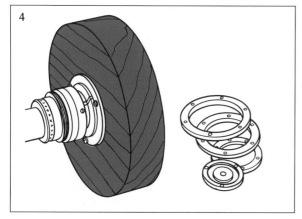

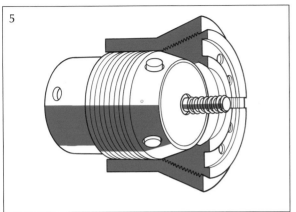

5

Large and small jaws can be added to the Masterchuck as shown. Screw chucks are formed by inserting a $\frac{5}{16}$in hexagonal bolt containing a central screw, or utilizing a metal faceplate which can fit either pin chucks or screw chucks. The inserted $\frac{5}{16}$in hexagonal bolt with the central screw is particularly useful where work has to be reversed on the face, for example, in picture frame production. A pilot hole of $\frac{1}{4}$in is drilled right through the work, and used from either side.

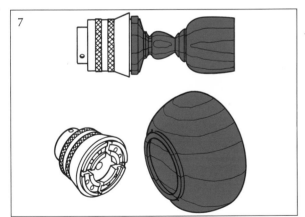

7

The versatility of wooden jaws made up as required by the woodturner is illustrated. These permit work on the base of any bowls, where initial or secondary means of holding may need to be removed. They will also facilitate remounting finished bowls for re-polishing. All these duplex chucks can be fitted with a suitably threaded base to accommodate any lathe.

Masterchuck (steps 5–8) This section illustrates the main features of the Henry Taylor Masterchuck, which has the same ability of the Multistar chuck to expand its jaws into a recess or compress them onto a dowel. In addition, wooden jaws can be attached which similarly expand and contract, (see step 8, below). In changing from expansion to compression mode, or vice versa, no change need be made in the chuck components.

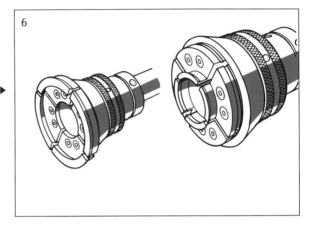

6

The range of ability to hold in expansion and compression is illustrated. The chuck will expand into a recess of 2¾in with standard jaws, or 3⅛in with the larger extension jaws. It will contract on to a spigot of 1⅜in diameter for standard jaws or 3⅛in for the larger extension jaws. The small 1¼in extension jaws will expand into a recess of 1½in and compress on a spigot of 1$\frac{5}{16}$in. All jaws have a maximum movement of ¼in on diameter.

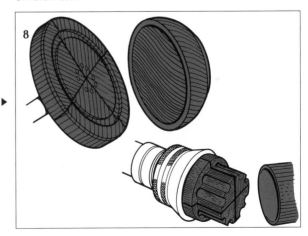

8

Produced by Axminster Power Tools, this is a self-centring, self-balancing chuck, and is a development of the engineering chuck. It is robust and heavy, the extra weight assisting in counteracting any out-of-balance movement leading to vibration. As with the Colchester Multistar chuck, it will run clockwise or anti-clockwise.

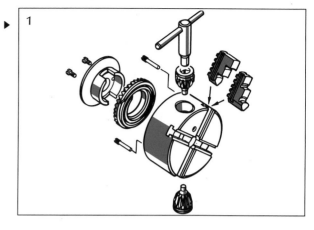

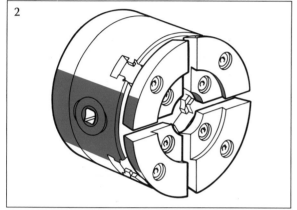

The dovetail bowl jaws replace the standard jaws supplied and provide secure mounting for large-diameter work. These jaws will grip internally and externally and can, therefore, be used into a recess or onto a spigot. The work can be re-mounted very accurately.

The wood jaw plates enable the turner to produce his own work-holding device. The plates can either act as a complement to the dovetail jaws, fitted in place of the actual dovetail segments, or can be fitted to their own set of chuck jaws. Grooves or recesses are turned on the wooden segments which will then either contract or expand to hold the work as required by the turner.

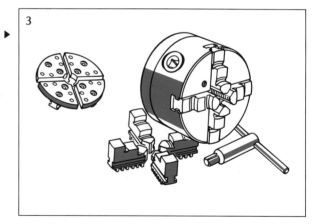

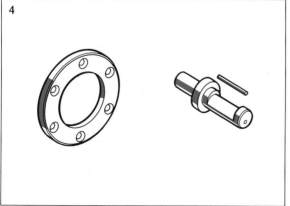

Faceplate rings can take the place of the traditional faceplate and can be used for a variety of operations, including the preparation of turning blanks for later operations. They can also be utilized in the mounting of wooden sanding discs, etc. Pin chucks in diameters $\frac{5}{8}$in, $\frac{3}{4}$in and $1\frac{1}{2}$in are available and are used for work holding where gripping or faceplate fixing is not practical.

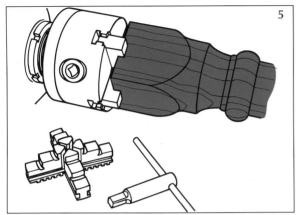

5

The chuck will hold square section wood utilizing the engineering pattern jaws. If these jaws protrude during this process a chuck guard is recommended or, alternatively, a strip of heavy-duty black fabric tape wrapped around the jaws. Both will make their presence obvious to the turner, and avoid injury to his knuckles.

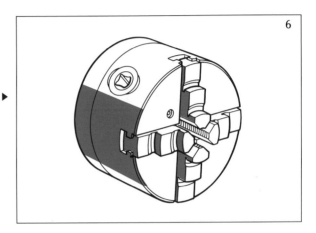

6

The chuck has a hollow centre to permit through boring, thus avoiding the necessity to turn the work 'end for end' to complete the boring. When fitted with the 'engineering' jaws as shown, very small diameter work can be securely held since the jaws close completely as the self-centring mechanism is wound in. In addition, there will be no need to prepare the work as the four jaws will firmly hold square work.

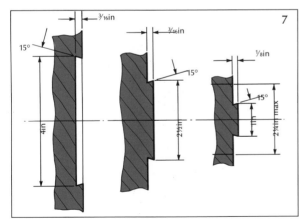

7

Work is held in compression using the four external jaws with diameters ranging from ⅛in to 1⅝in. Dovetail jaws size 'A' will work in compression at 1in and 2½in diameters. Dovetail jaws size 'B' will hold work in compression at 1in only. When working in compression, the jaws hold work firmly to 10in lengths unsupported by a tail centre.

For holding work in expansion, in addition to the four internal jaws, the dovetail bowl jaws size 'A' will hold in expansion at 4in and the dovetail bowl jaws size 'B' at 2½in. This method of holding ensures a large area is in contact with the work around the circumference of the jaws. Work can be readily removed and re-positioned without losing concentricity.

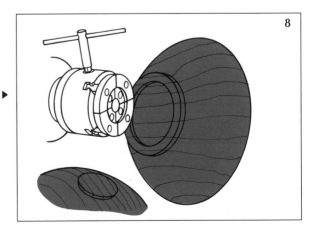

8

It is important to have a bowl shape in mind before work starts on the blank. It is not enough to expect that inspiration will come as you turn the wood. Inspiration will certainly come, but usually about two minutes after you have just turned away the bit of wood you want to keep. Some very good designs of bowl arise from faults in the wood or, occasionally, faults in the toolwork by the turner.

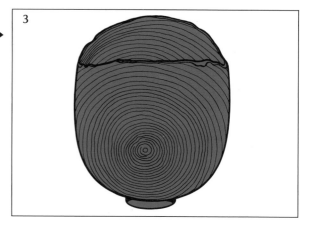

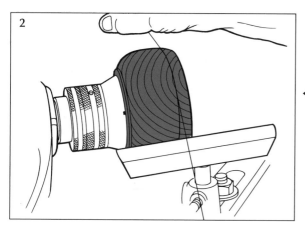

For all turning decoration, V-notches to various depths, beading in various sizes, and hot-wire decoration are suitable. Hot-wire decoration is made by making a small nick with the toe of a skew chisel and then holding a piece of stainless steel wire between toggles firmly onto the nick until friction causes the wood to burn, giving a black line.

Bark-edged, or waney-edged as they are sometimes known, bowls provide their own decoration. In many cases the beauty of the figuring in the wood would not be enhanced by applied decoration. A work can easily be spoiled by over-decoration. If in doubt, leave the wood to speak for itself.

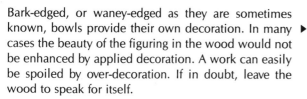

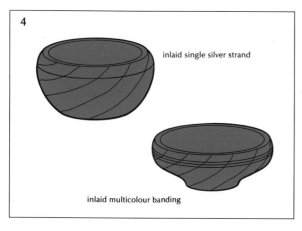

In dark woods, an inlay of silver wire below the rim can be effective. In light or dark woods, an inlay of contrasting banding is attractive. Copper or silver applied to a bowl surface can give an interesting effect.

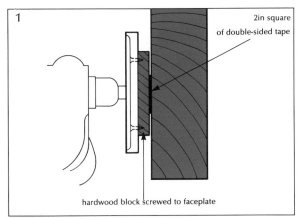

Single chucking means that the work is mounted on the lathe face; all turning is done in that one position and the work is finished and taken off as a finished article. It is quick, but it does not allow a great deal of scope for fancy design. Single chucking can be achieved with double-sided tape on a wood block mounted on a faceplate.

Another very popular method of single chucking is to use one of the many screw chucks available to turn and finish an article and then, having removed it from the lathe, fill the hole left by the screw chuck. In this case, the length of the screw of the screw chuck will determine the thickness of, for example, the bowl bottom, and it may be necessary to 'washer up' the screw with hardboard or plywood discs.

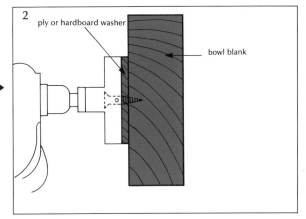

Double chucking involves mounting the work with its best face to the lathe, turning the underneath part of the article and allowing for a spigot or recess which will be used in the second part of the operation – double chucking. The operation can be started with double-sided tape to the best face mounted to a wood block on a faceplate, or it can be the best face being held by a pin chuck or screw chuck.

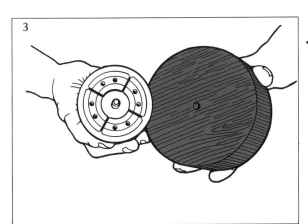

The second operation in double chucking can be completed with the jaws of one of the duplex or combination chucks, or the four-jaw self-centring chuck in either expansion or contraction.

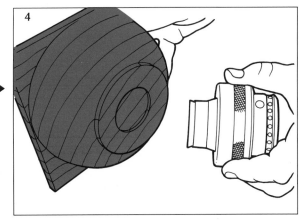

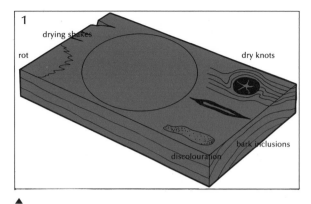

1

drying shakes
rot
dry knots
discolouration
bark inclusions

▲

Plane both faces of the work before cutting out the bowl blank. It is very difficult to see faults in a sawn surface of the wood and, of course, it will be necessary to have a flat face for mounting to the lathe.

Examine for faults in the wood on both faces. Faults need not lead to the bowl blank being rejected, but they ▶ will have an effect on the final design of the bowl. Determine which will be the best face, i.e. the one which will be hollowed out and facing upwards. Mark out with a pencil and compasses, and punch the centre of the best face.

Band-saw around the blank or use a circular saw to cut the blank to an octagonal. A bowl can readily be turned ▶ down to a disc from an octagonal, but it is not advisable to try to turn down to a disc from the square. Provided that the saw cut does not touch the outerline of the blank, great accuracy is not needed.

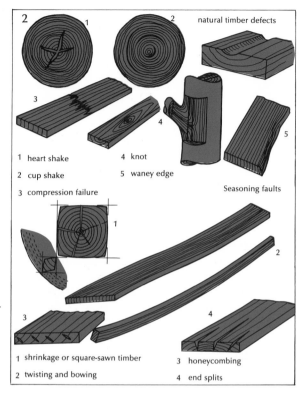

2 natural timber defects

1 heart shake   4 knot
2 cup shake   5 waney edge
3 compression failure

Seasoning faults

1 shrinkage or square-sawn timber   3 honeycombing
2 twisting and bowing   4 end splits

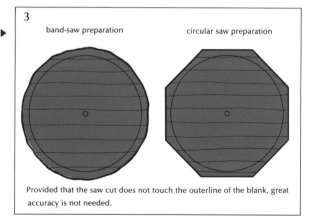

3

band-saw preparation   circular saw preparation

Provided that the saw cut does not touch the outerline of the blank, great accuracy is not needed.

Re-examine the blank for bark inclusions or hidden ◀ defects now exposed as the sides have been sawn. Again, this need not necessarily lead to rejection of the blank, but one should be aware of any faults which will affect the design and, in the case of a serious flaw in the wood which could affect stability, the blank ought to be rejected.

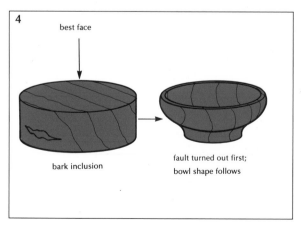

4

best face

bark inclusion

fault turned out first;
bowl shape follows

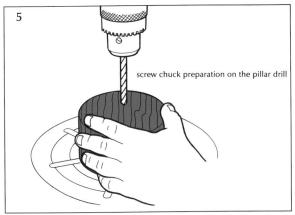

5

screw chuck preparation on the pillar drill

Mount the work to the faceplate, either with double-sided tape or by screwing into the bowl blank (the screw holes will be removed when the bowl blank is reversed in double chucking). Alternatively, a screw chuck or pin chuck can be used.

Using a ⅜in or ½in bowl gouge of the deep-fluted long and strong pattern, round the blank to a disc without attempting any further shaping. Notice that where the grain runs directly against the cutting edge of the tool it is rougher on two opposite sides of the disc due to the fact that the turner is cutting into end-grain. Should any sore spots appear in the work subsequently, they will almost always be found in this end-grain.

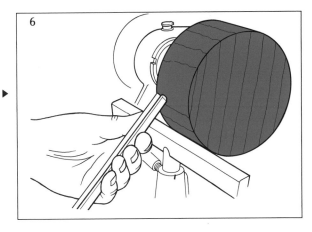

6

Moving the rest to fit across the base of the bowl blank, flat the base using the ⅜in or ½in bowl gouge as shown, the bevel rubbing, the handle high, and the tool on its side and moving straight into the centre.

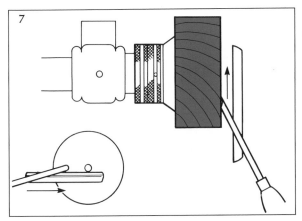

7

The base of the bowl is now prepared for re-mounting, either by forming a spigot or a recess. Various patterns are shown for mounting in the Multistar, the Masterchuck, the combination chuck or the four-jaw self-centring chuck.

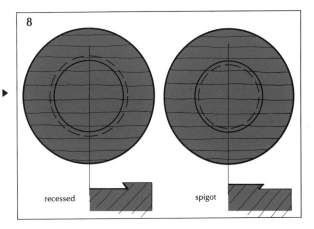

8

recessed   spigot

The recess to hold jaws in expansion is started by the parting tool, cutting to a depth of ⅛in. The cut is ▶ repeated on the inside in order to give room for the bowl gouge to take out the waste to the centre of the base. If a spigot is required for jaws in contraction, it is outlined with the parting tool, and the bowl gouge is used on its side, the bevel rubbing to remove waste outwards.

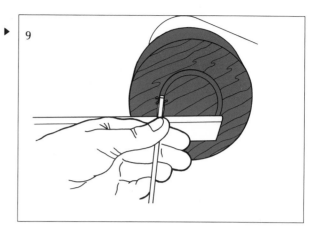

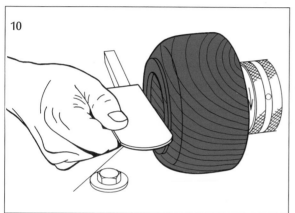

A straight edge is used to ensure that both the recess and ◀ the spigot have flat or slightly concave bases to guarantee stability when standing. When turning a bowl on the outside, always work to the outside, and work with the bowl gouge on its side, the bevel rubbing and moving around the outside of the base towards the bowl wall.

The shaping of the exterior of the bowl continues with the bowl gouge, starting to take off where the maximum ▶ must be removed, thus producing tapers where the turner wishes to shape the exterior surfaces.

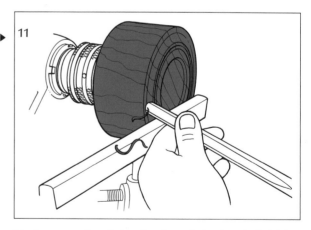

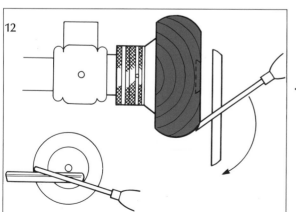

Having completed the shaping of the bowl, finishing ◀ cuts are made on any surface which requires improvement (*see* pages 30 and 31). The rest is removed and the exterior surface is sanded, first with 120-grit, then with 180 grit. Apply Danish oil, teak oil, tung oil, or salad oil by rag, then polish. Alternatively use paste wax (Briwax), applied by hand or brush, then polished.

13

Abrasives in turning

1. Always remove the rest before turning.
2. Always sand from underneath.
3. Use abrasives in sequence 120-grit, 180-grit and finish with either 240-grit or 0000 wire wool.

The sequence of operations in all turning is as follows: shaping, finishing cuts, sanding and decoration. Decoration follows sanding because if it were done beforehand the sanding operation would blur the sharp outlines of any decoration made.

Polishing techniques vary considerably. Three methods are given here to form a basis on which the student may build and experiment. A gloss finish with a non-slip surface can be obtained by using cellulose sanding sealer brushed on thinly, allowed to dry (four minutes), given five seconds abrasion with wire wool (0000 grade), and then burnished with a handful of shavings in the hand of the turner. At this point the hand with the shavings should be kept moving to avoid burning either the work or the hand.

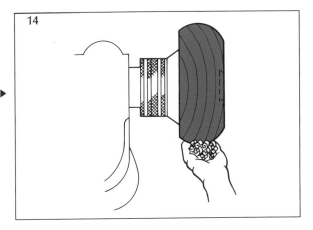

14

A second method provides a good shine with a waxed finish which could be used for an exhibition piece. Carry out the three operations as listed in step 14 above and then apply a Liberon turner's stick (which is made up of Carnauba wax and resin) over the surface of the turning work once only. Bring to a shine with a soft cloth held single thickness with a single finger pressing firmly in order to melt the wax.

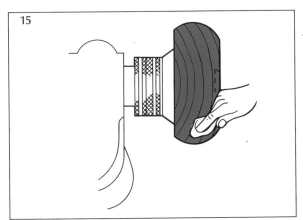

15

Thirdly, Danish oil or teak oil can be applied by rag or brush to the unsealed wood and driven in by friction from the polishing cloth. Alternatively, a paste wax, such as Briwax, can be applied with the work stationary, with the bare hand, until it becomes tacky (two to three minutes) when it is given a polish with the work rotating in the lathe.

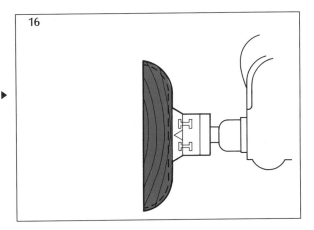

16

The bowl is now mounted to the duplex chuck and without change of speed, the work is checked for ▶ accurate running. Modern chucks will mount and re-mount bowl blanks with consistent accuracy and minimum movement out of true. Such movement as may arise will be caused by the slight crushing of the wood fibres by the jaws in either expansion or contraction.

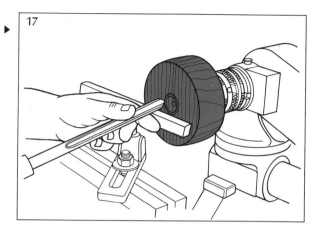

At a distance, generally of 4–8in from the centre of the bowl, there is a tendency for the bowl gouge to be ▶ thrown out to the side. This is known as 'centrifuging out' and can be prevented by turning the rest into the hollow of the bowl already made. (Only the top ½in of the bowl rim is at risk from this centrifuging out; once below ½in the gouge can be used in the traditional classic bowl cut as illustrated).

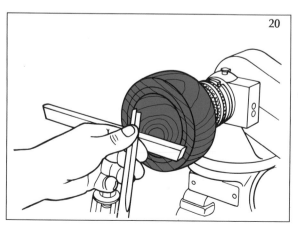

◀ The bowl is hollowed out to depth using a ⅜in bowl gouge. Initially the rest runs across the centre of the bowl and the bowl gouge movement is as shown. A depth gauge is made from dowel and scrap, as shown, to ensure easy checking of the bowl blank for correct depth.

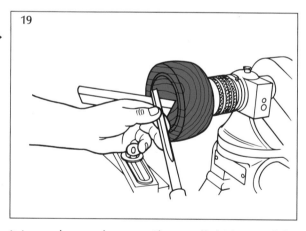

◀ It is usual to work to a uniform wall thickness of the bowl. This is most easily achieved, not with callipers, but with the left-hand thumb inside the bowl, the fingers outside to sense any slight change in thickness. At this stage it is advisable to make 'one cut followed by one finger stroke'. In all turning do not take any more cuts than you have to; it is always the last cut you make that lets you down.

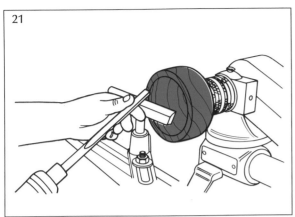

21

The lip of the bowl is finished with the bowl gouge, as shown, passing across it from outside to inside. The lip may be angled in towards the centre of the bowl, or may be flat; it could be rounded or, indeed, beaded.

With the bowl stationary, examine for sore spots, raised grain, or any damage that will require a finishing cut to repair. Do not attempt to sand out such damage, as the affected area is usually much deeper than at first appears and will take a long time to clear. Use finishing cuts as shown on pages 30 and 31 and reduce the time spent sanding to an absolute minimum.

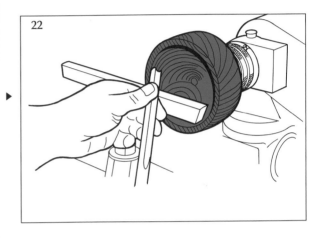

22

Choose the finishing process of your preference from page 45 or experiment with your own ideas. It is not practicable to leave the bowl untreated, as it will rapidly become dirty with handling and will need protection of some sort.

23

Oiled Finishes

For any item in contact with food, use pure mineral oil (liquid paraffin) – obtainable from chemists as a laxative. All other wooden articles, Tung, Danish or teak oil.

First application – dilute with 10 per cent white spirit. Apply with cloth and burnish with wire wool until dry.

Second application – undiluted as above. Wire wool and finish with a soft cloth.

With finishing complete, the bowl can be dismounted from the chuck and checked for stability on its base. If the bowl is intended as a present, pyrography in the recess can be used to indicate the name of the wood used and the initials of the maker. Details of pyrography pens are given in Appendix 5, page 125.

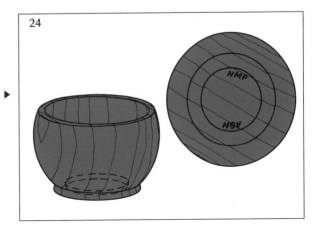

24

This exercise practises drilling and the use of callipers on the lathe. The sketch gives suitable dimensions but these can be altered to suit the turner's requirements, whether he is making a bradawl or a lathe tool handle. The material can be sweet chestnut, ash or beech.

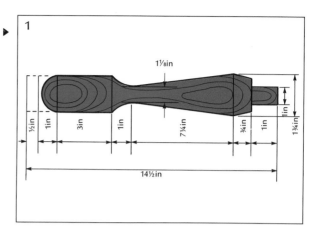

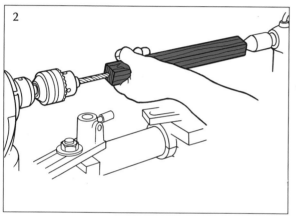

The hole for the blade tang is drilled, as shown in step 4, page 28, with the wood in the square. This permits 'turning around the hole' to ensure final concentricity. For convenience, a Jacob's chuck is mounted in the headstock and the speed is reduced to the minimum. The handle is removed after drilling and re-fitted with the normal twin-prong driving head with the drilled hole fitting into the tailstock. The work is roughed down using a roughing gouge (see page 20).

The callipers are set to the outside of the ferrule, and two calliper dimensions cut with a parting tool (full details of this procedure can be found on page 26). The ferrule is fitted to an interference fit by careful use of the ⅜in beading tool (see step 4, page 30).

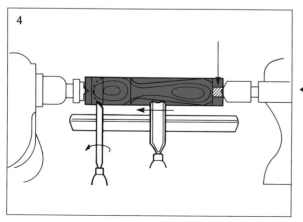

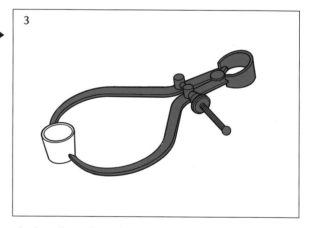

The handle is shaped using a 1½in roughing gouge and the butt end of the handle is shaped to a comfortable handgrip using the toe of a skew chisel. Remember that when using the roughing gouge for shaping, it is still necessary to keep the blade at right angles to the work, as shown in the illustration. Attempts to come to the work at an angle will usually result in corrugations forming on the work.

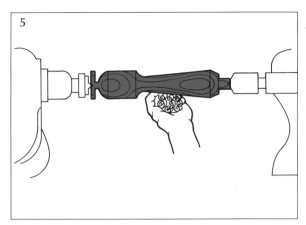

The handle will be given a non-slip burnished finish, as illustrated in step 14, page 18). At least ¼in of material is left at the end of the handle to provide strength during this finishing process. Use any shavings for burnishing, taking care to keep the hand moving throughout to avoid burning. Five second's burnishing time is quite sufficient, and there should be no change in speed for this treatment.

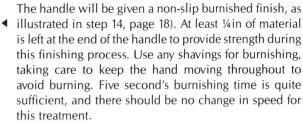

When burnishing is complete, the handle can be parted from the lathe using a junior hack-saw, as shown in the illustration. Note that the operation will be one-handed with the hack-saw, because the left hand will be supporting the work to catch it when it has parted through.

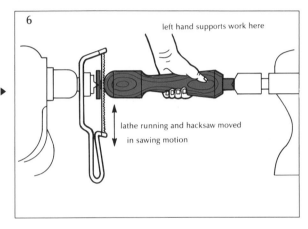

left hand supports work here

lathe running and hacksaw moved in sawing motion

left hand supporting work here

skew chisel deepening V-cut to part off

An alternative method of parting off is to continue cutting the V-notch with the parting tool single-handed, while the other hand supports the work and catches it when parting is complete. This method will give a more rounded finish but it may take longer.

The tool blade is fitted by setting it upside-down in a vice and using a mallet to drive the handle onto the tang of the blade. It is advisable to use a simple adhesive to ensure that the blade stays firm in the handle.

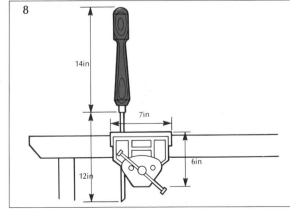

14in

7in

12in

6in

This is an exercise in long hole boring, between centre turning and face turning. Full details of the technique of long hole boring are to be found on page 29. The three essentials to remember are that the speed should be the lowest of which the lathe is capable, the long hole boring auger must be held with the trough upright (both in insertion and retraction), and the depth of drilling should not exceed 1in for each pass.

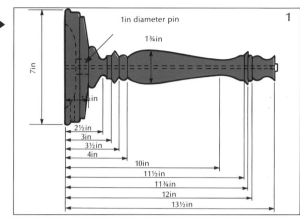

1

1in diameter pin

1¾in

7in

⅜in

2½in
3in
3½in
4in
10in
11½in
11¾in
12in
13½in

The wooden standard is bored in the square to ensure that the hole will be in the centre when it is turned between centres. The dimensioned sketch shows the finished article, method of assembly, fitting of the threaded nipple and additional drilling required in the hollowed-out base. The bored standard is placed between centres, with the top in the tailstock. The work is driven by a $\frac{5}{16}$in counter-bore.

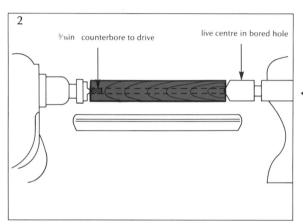

2

⁵⁄₁₆in counterbore to drive

live centre in bored hole

After roughing down, the work is set out by pencil using a simple pattern stick (*see* step 4, page 25). Do not, at this stage, use copy turning techniques, which will be dealt with in a later example, but use the tools as indicated in the sketch to form the shapes of the standard, judging by eye the the curves and diameters required. Provided that the turner looks at the back profile throughout the turning operation, the eye can be relied upon as a very good comparer.

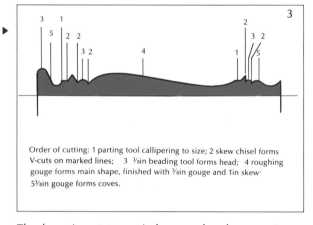

3

3 1
5 2 2
   3 2

2
3 2
1 5

4

Order of cutting: 1 parting tool callipering to size; 2 skew chisel forms V-cuts on marked lines; 3 ⅜in beading tool forms head; 4 roughing gouge forms main shape, finished with ⅜in gouge and 1in skew· 5 ⅜in gouge forms coves.

The base is cut to a circle on a band-saw or to an octagon on a circular saw. The work is most conveniently mounted on a screw chuck and, since the work has to be turned on both faces, a suitable diameter hole is drilled in the centre, right through the work.

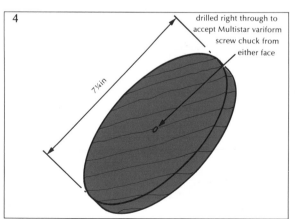

4

drilled right through to accept Multistar variform screw chuck from either face

7¼in

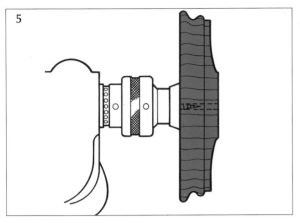

5

The work is reversed and hollowed underneath using the ⅜in bowl gouge. Ensure that sufficient material is hollowed out from the base to allow the $\frac{5}{16}$in cable access hole to be drilled from the side. At this stage both the standard and the base can be prepared for finishing with a coat of sanding sealer.

◀ The base is mounted to the screw chuck and rounded to a disc. The top of the base is shaped with a ⅜in bowl gouge. Take care that the part of the base that will support the standard is smooth and slightly dished in, so that no joint will be visible. This will also ensure that when the work is reversed, it will be accurately positioned on the screw chuck.

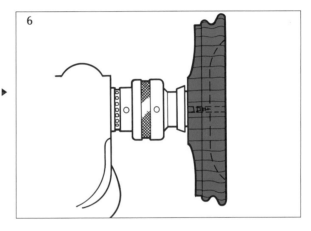

6

◀ When the sealer is dry, the base is drilled to accept the three-core electric cable but the centre is not drilled out to accept the standard spigot until the work has been re-mounted, wire-wooled, burnished and, if required, waxed, before removal from the lathe.

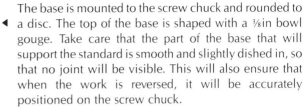

7

hand or power drill with ⁵⁄₁₆in bit

direction of grain

The final fitting involves screwing the brass threaded nipple into the top of the work, threading the cable ▶ through both the standard and the base and fitting the electric cable to the bulb holder and plug. Finally, adhesive needs to be added to the pin and socket joint and both parts pressed firmly together.

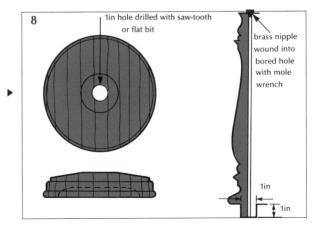

8

1in hole drilled with saw-tooth or flat bit

brass nipple wound into bored hole with mole wrench

1in

1in

This is an exercise in the use of the skew chisel. However, a number of different tools could be used to make the same article. The sketch shows a finished mouse in the usual size when cut from odd left-over scraps of material, but the mouse can be any size from 1in diameter to 4in. The body is made from any suitable offcut, the ears are brown felt and the tail is a leather strip.

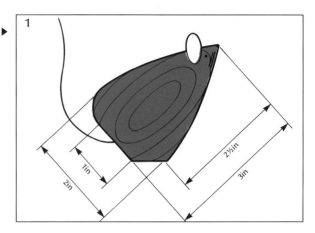

The material is mounted between centres, roughed down to a cylinder and given a planing cut to both the left and right to produce a fine smooth finish. This cut with the heel of the skew chisel leading will give a fine finish to any wood, including softwood.

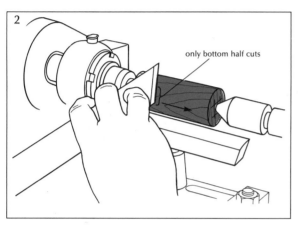

The body of the mouse is marked out with the work running and a diamond-shaped parting tool is used to cut to half-way through outside either line. The material outside the line, to left and right, is waste.

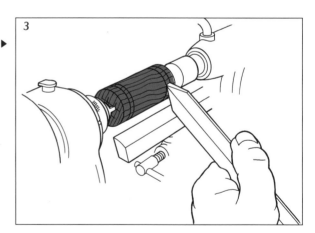

The base of the mouse is rounded using the heel of the skew. The tool must be sharp and should be held firmly in a rolling action giving shavings and a fine finish. Avoid any tendency to hold the skew flat thereby producing a scraped finish. This will rapidly remove the good edge from the tool and result in a very poor finish on the work.

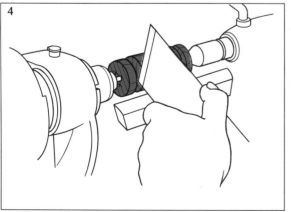

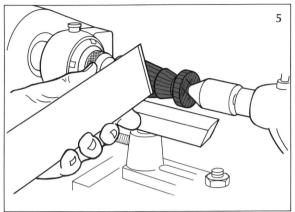

5

The nose of the mouse is tapered with the skew chisel, with the heel leading. As usual, the material must be taken off first where the maximum has to be removed. The skew chisel continues to taper down until ¼in material is left between centres at the nose.

No finish is required on this article and if the cuts have been made correctly, no sanding should be required either. However, if there are any imperfections, remove the rest and sand lightly to finish. The work is parted off using a junior hack-saw for speed and convenience, with the left hand supporting the work; the lathe can be running or stationary.

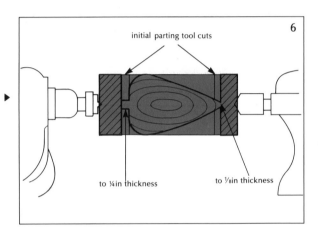

6

initial parting tool cuts

to ¼in thickness

to ⅛in thickness

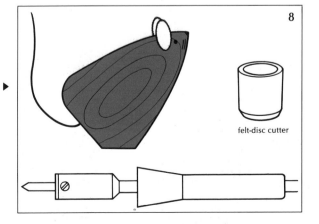

7

CL

sand

Flats are sanded on the mouse after the nose has been removed either by hack-saw or band-saw. The mouse can either be kept in this shape as a child's toy, or it can be drilled to accept a ¼in dowel 1in long on the bottom, sanded flat. This is glued in to place, and a corresponding hole drilled at the side of a cheese board. The mouse is then an optional decoration at the side of the board.

Using a pyrography tool, the eyes, nose (and, if necessary, whiskers) are added. The ears are punched out of scrap felt using a sharpened piece of piping and the tail is cut from a leather thong. Ears and tail are secured with hot-melt glue and the exercise is complete.

8

felt-disc cutter

The illustration shows two ways of forming a lidded box. Both methods will be used for this exercise. The hollowing out of the box and lid will be in end-grain and will, therefore, require very sharp tools and extra pressure. The purpose of the exercise is to practise tight lid fitting so that there is definite air pressure and suction when the lid is inserted or removed.

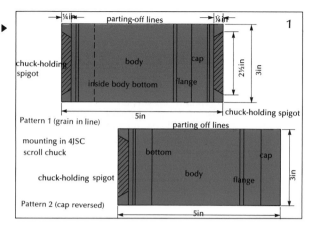

Pattern 1 (grain in line)

mounting in 4JSC scroll chuck

chuck-holding spigot

Pattern 2 (cap reversed)

The blank is prepared as shown for mounting in combination, duplex or scroll chucks. Mounting in a screw chuck is not recommended since holding in end-grain is not secure. Preparation for mounting is completed between centres. The blank is mounted to the selected chuck and marked out as shown while still rotating.

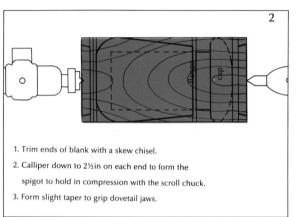

1. Trim ends of blank with a skew chisel.

2. Calliper down to 2½in on each end to form the spigot to hold in compression with the scroll chuck.

3. Form slight taper to grip dovetail jaws.

The lid of the box is parted off with a diamond-shaped parting tool at the point shown. The parting tool is held one-handed, in the right hand, the left hand supporting and catching the box lid. An alternative method, removing less waste and therefore giving a better grain match, is with the hack-saw and this technique is shown in step 6, page 49.

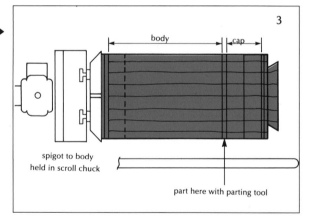

spigot to body held in scroll chuck

part here with parting tool

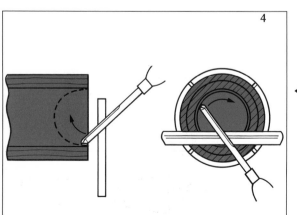

Since this box is not cylindrical, but is tapered toward the lip, the marking of the top of the box allows for the taper and for the wall thickness. The box is hollowed from the front using a ⅜in bowl gouge and a ¼in long and strong bowl gouge. Note the angle of the gouge for starting the cut for deep hollowing. A depth gauge is used to ensure that the correct depth is obtained.

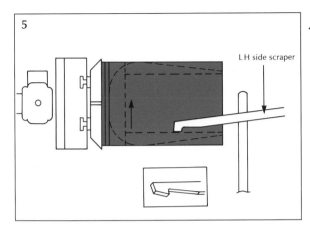

First method (steps 5–12)   A square-edged or left-hand side scraper is used to finish the inside and bottom of the box. It is essential that the first ½in of the box is absolutely vertical and without taper. The good fit of the lid will depend upon this. The finish of the bottom and the walls of the box should be good enough to require no sanding; sanding inside the box will invite 'bell mouthing' and should be avoided.

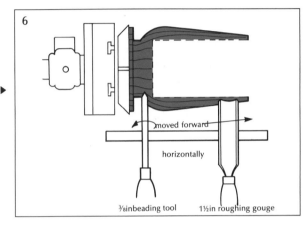

The outside of the box is shaped to a taper using a 1½in roughing gouge and rounded at the base using a ⅜in beading tool. The outside of the box is sanded and both the outside and inside are finished using sanding sealer, wire wool and wax. The box is not parted from the lathe but is dismounted by unscrewing the chuck.

The lid is now mounted in place of the box and callipers are set to slightly wider than the box aperture. The flange on the lid is callipered down to diameter using a parting tool in two places and the waste is removed with the 1½in roughing gouge.

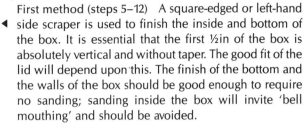

The lid is fitted to the box by careful use of the ⅜in beading tool in a planing cut with the box being offered up between each cut until a smooth sliding fit is achieved. Do not attempt to use sandpaper at this stage as it is difficult to obtain a flat finish and it will remove an unknown quantity of material.

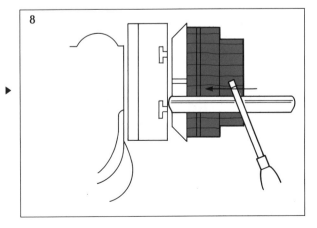

The interior of the lid is hollowed using the ⅜in bowl gouge working from outside to inside. The rest will be ▶ in the normal position, approximately ¾in below the centre of axis.

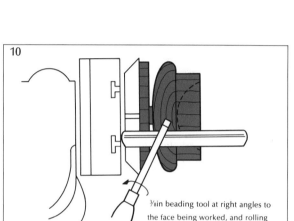

9

plan view   side view

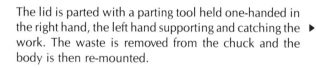

The lid is parted with a parting tool held one-handed in the right hand, the left hand supporting and catching the ▶ work. The waste is removed from the chuck and the body is then re-mounted.

⅜in beading tool at right angles to
the face being worked, and rolling
over to the left.

◀ The lid top is shaped using the ⅜in beading tool or the toe of the skew chisel. Note the necessity to move the rest to accommodate the curve of the lid top. The lid is then sanded in every part except the flange and finished in the usual manner.

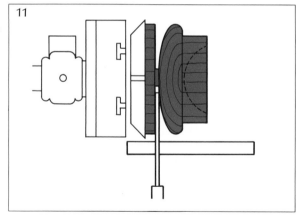

11

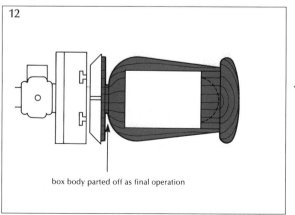

12

box body parted off as final operation

◀ With the body re-mounted and the lid fitted, final sanding of the lid can be completed, followed by sanding sealer, wire wool and wax over the whole interior and exterior of the box and its lid. The lid is removed and placed on one side and the body parted off in the usual way with a parting tool.

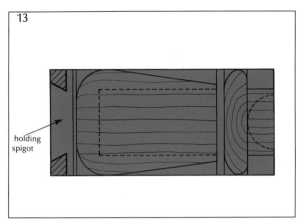

13

holding
spigot

The wood blank is placed between centres, roughed down to a cylinder and marked out as shown. One end ▶ is prepared for fitting into a duplex or scroll chuck. It is recommended that the box body should not be made too deep because this may cause difficulties in obtaining a good inside surface. 2in to 2½in would seem to be a convenient body length.

Second method (steps 13–20) This is an alternative ◀ method of making a lidded box, where only one end of the blank is prepared for holding in the chuck. The disadvantage of this method is that the lid is reversed and the grain does not match the body of the box.

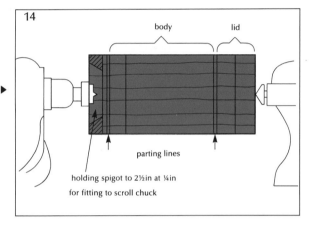

14

body   lid

parting lines

holding spigot to 2½in at ¼in
for fitting to scroll chuck

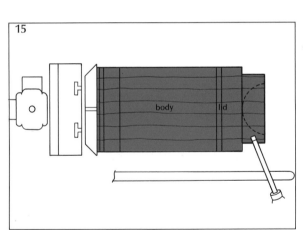

15

body   lid

The top of the lid is partially formed and then the whole is sanded, except for the flange where care is taken in its ▶ final cutting to be sure that it is flat and without any taper. Sanding sealer and finishing process is applied and then the lid is parted off in the usual way.

The flange is cut in the lid with a parting tool and the ◀ inside of the lid hollowed with a ⅜in bowl gouge. Unless the box is to be of very small dimensions, hollowing the lid will improve the capacity of the box and also lighten it.

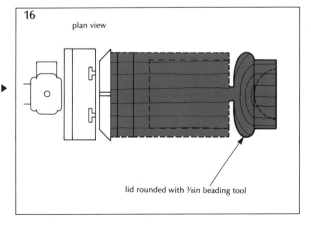

16

plan view

lid rounded with ⅜in beading tool

The box body is hollowed out using a ⅜in bowl gouge and a ¼in bowl gouge as in the previous example. Do not attempt to hollow out the box using a scraper. Scrapers should only be used for finishing cuts. ▶

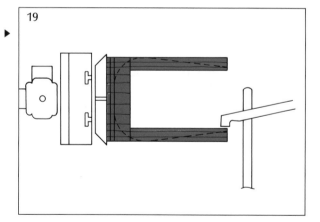

17

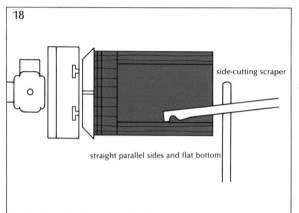

18

side-cutting scraper

straight parallel sides and flat bottom

◀ A sharp square, or left-edged scraper is used to finish the inside wall and the bottom of the box. Again, care must be taken to ensure that the first ½in from the lip downward is flat and without taper.

The fitting of the lid is not quite as straightforward in this example, in that final cuts must be taken with a sharp scraper on the inside of the box until the lid is a tight sliding fit in the box body. The final shaping of the box is completed as in the previous example using a roughing gouge on the taper and the ⅜in beading tool for the bottom rounding of the box. ▶

19

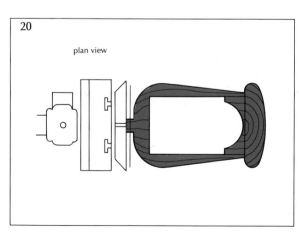

20

plan view

◀ The box is sanded externally and then finished, both internally and externally, with sanding sealer and wire wool. Then it is polished. The lid is re-mounted for final finishing on its top. Should the lid be a slack fit a paper tissue will jam the lid to permit work to continue. Finally, the box body is parted off in the usual way.

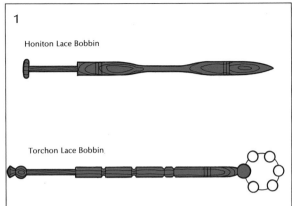

1

Honiton Lace Bobbin

Torchon Lace Bobbin

Two patterns of lace bobbins are shown: the Honiton Lace Bobbin and the Midlands Bobbin (sometimes called the Torchon Lace Bobbin). The Honiton is used to weave in and out of the threads and, therefore, has a pointed nose. The Midland, or Torchon, is used with a heavier grade of cotton and requires the the addition of spangles in glass beads to tension the heavier material. It is essential to both patterns that there be no rough parts or points on which the cotton can snag.

The bobbins can be made from any close-grained wood – holly would be ideal for the beginner. A blank should be cut ⅜in square and 6in long, mounted in a three-jaw Jacob's chuck with the tail centre replaced by a long dead centre. This will permit the rest to be moved very close to the work.

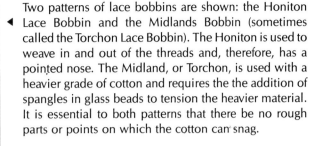

2

The bobbin blank is roughed down using a 1½in roughing gouge and it is advisable to do the bulk of the wood removal at this stage since it will save time later. It may seem heavy-handed to use the large 1½in roughing gouge on this thin work, but the turner will find that the large gouge reduces vibration and quickly brings the work into the round, and then down to the required diameter.

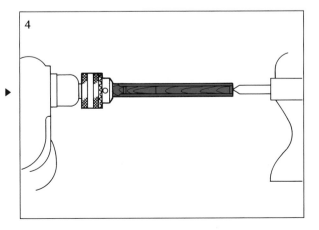

3

1½in roughing gouge at right angles to bobbin blank.

The blank is set out as shown and the sequence of turning is from the tailstock end to the driving head so that no narrow sections are overstressed. As an aid to setting out, a pin gauge is used (see page 25) to ensure that all bobbins are of identical dimensions, and to speed up the work.

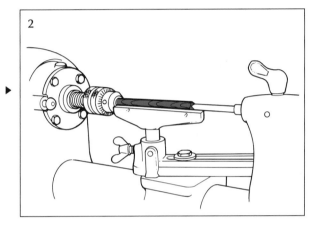

4

Honiton (steps 5–8)   The point of the bobbin is shaped using either a skew chisel or the ⅜in beading tool. ▶ Whichever tool is used, the left hand supports behind the work and the right hand holds the tool. Care should be taken to ensure that pressure for cutting is exerted along the bobbin rather than across it. This will reduce bending and vibration in the work.

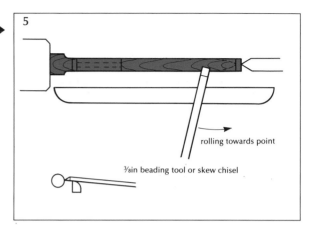

The neck is the thinnest part of the bobbin and requires ◀ the use of the smallest parting tool available. It is possible to adapt a carpenter's chisel for this purpose, as shown. The neck is marked out with the point of the skew chisel and the waste removed either with the modified carpenter's chisel or with a ¼in or ⅜in beading tool. Throughout all these operations, the tool is held in the right hand whilst the left hand supports the bobbin. The head is cut with the carpenter's chisel as illustrated.

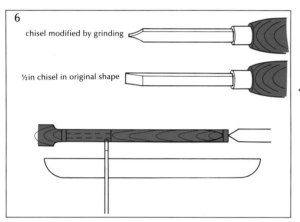

The bobbin is sanded throughout with 180-grit abrasive and decoration is applied, usually in the form of V- ▶ notches and beads. Carnauba wax is run along the work and then melted onto it using finger and thumb. (This avoids the use of a cloth which could catch the bobbin and possibly break it.)

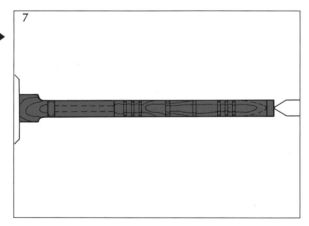

The tailstock end is parted off first and the point of the ◀ bobbin is parted using a skew chisel in the usual manner. The pointed tip can then be sanded whilst running, and re-waxed. The head of the bobbin is parted off using the carpenter's chisel or a parting tool in the usual manner.

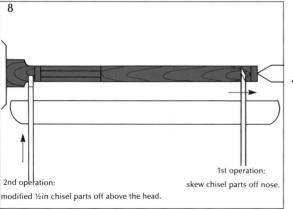

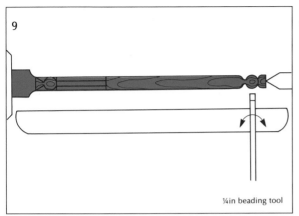

¼in beading tool

The neck is made in the same manner as in step 6, page 60. The thistle head on this pattern of bobbin is the second main difference between the Torchon and the Honiton Lace Bobbin. The thistle head is formed using a carpenter's chisel or a parting tool. The bobbin is sanded, paying particular attention to the neck, then waxed and polished. Alternatively, the work can be finished with coloured Briwax, applied by hand and polished with paper tissue, or french polish applied and dried, whilst running, with a soft cloth.

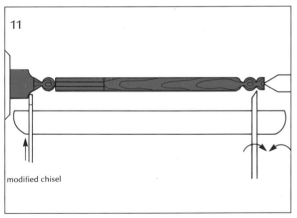

modified chisel

The illustration shows the method of fitting the spangles to the ball. Spangles can be obtained from bobbin-blank suppliers or, occasionally, from the glass beads of Victorian necklaces found on street stalls. A list of bobbin suppliers is given in Appendix 6, page 125. Conventionally, the spangle is made up of five or seven glass beads, the number depending on their size.

Torchon (steps 9–12)   After roughing down, the bobbin pattern is set out with the work revolving and the ball at the spangle end is turned with a ¼in beading tool or a skew chisel. This bobbin uses a heavier cotton than the Honiton Lace Bobbin, and requires the heavier weight of the coloured glass spangle mounted on brass wire running through the turned ball.

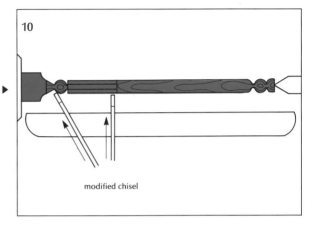

modified chisel

The ball is parted from the tailstock using the skew chisel or a hack-saw and it is sanded and re-waxed. The head is parted using either a parting tool or a hack-saw. In either case, the work is lightly held in the left hand while the right hand parts through.

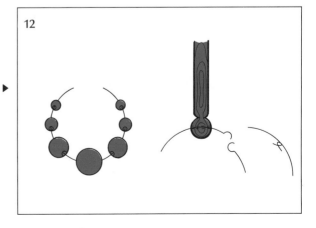

KITCHEN SCOOP

These useful kitchen items come in a variety of shapes and sizes, from the small salt scoop to the larger flour and sugar scoops. The smaller scoops are usually made in one piece. Larger scoops are more conveniently made in two pieces with the handle dowelled into the scoop bowl.

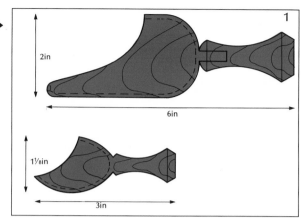

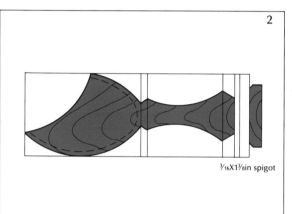

Ideal woods for kitchen equipment are sycamore, beech or elm. The illustration shows a small scoop set out on a turned blank, prepared for holding in a Masterchuck by a small spigot. It is not advisable to attempt to turn multiple scoops from one blank since vibration will lead to inaccurate wall thickness and a poor finish.

It is possible to hold the work in either the duplex chucks, (the Masterchuck and the Multistar), a cup chuck, a split-ring or split-collet chuck or in a four-jaw self-centring chuck. The illustration shows the blanks prepared for alternative mountings.

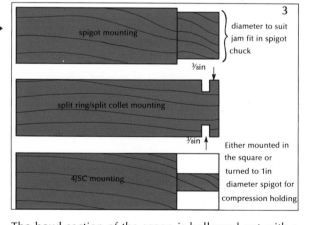

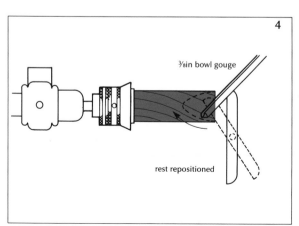

The bowl section of the scoop is hollowed out with a ⅜in bowl gouge to the shape shown, and sanded. Since this hollowing is in end-grain, considerable pressure will be required. In addition, take care that once the initial hollowing is started, the gouge is put to the interior wall of the scoop as near right angles as possible, if necessary re-positioning the rest.

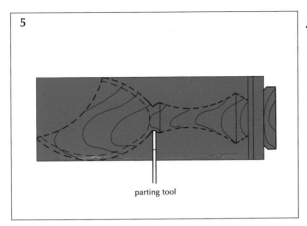

5

parting tool

In shaping the outside of the bowl it is important that the bowl thickness is uniform and that the outside profile matches that of the inside. Use a parting tool as shown to find the correct depth and bowl thickness before shaping the bottom part of the bowl. Shape the handle using the ⅜in bowl gouge with a ½in skew chisel for decoration. Part off with either a junior hack-saw or a parting tool after finishing with sanding sealer, wire wool and a coat of Danish oil.

If the scoop is to be made in two parts, shape the bottom of the bowl as shown to form a spigot; the top of the handle is drilled to fit the spigot. Scoops do not require any means of hanging as they are best stored inside the salt, sugar or flour containers for which they are intended.

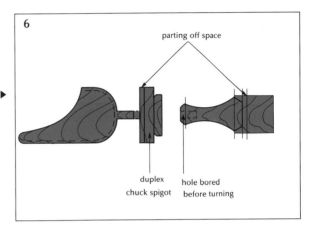

6

parting off space

duplex chuck spigot

hole bored before turning

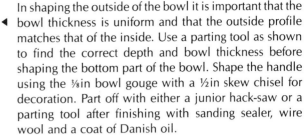

7

Feed to saw blade.

L/C

block with tapered hollow,
cut in half for strong compression grip

Mark the outside of the scoop with a pencil line to show where it is to be cut to its final shape on the band-saw. Hold the work firmly and feed it into the saw slowly. If a large number are to be made, it would add to convenience and safety if a simple jig were made for this operation.

An alternative method of shaping the scoop is to use a sanding disc made up from a faceplate and scrap wood with 120-grit paper glued to the face. An 8in disc is adequate for most purposes and it will permit good control of the shape when sanding. A soft cylinder sander (felt, plastic foam or foam rubber with an abrasive loop) running from either a drill or a lathe is ideal for this operation.

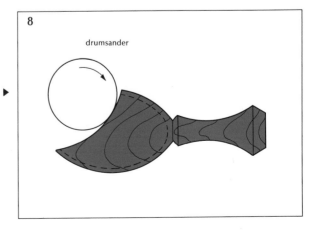

8

drumsander

The sketch shows the usual pattern of salt spoon used with a table cruet. This exercise is included because it ▶ illustrates a fairly unconventional method of attachment of work to the faceplate. The spoon is turned in two stages. First it is turned between centres to form the handle and the ball on the end and, second, it is re-mounted on the faceplate to hollow out the ball to form a scoop.

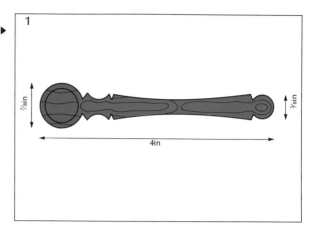

The work is turned between centres to produce the ◀ profile as shown, with the tools as indicated in the sketch. At this stage, the work is given a coat of sanding sealer and burnished, since it will not be re-mounted between centres after the scoop has been turned out.

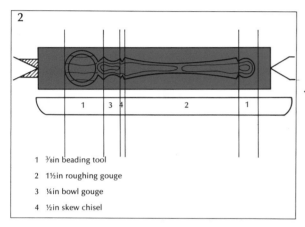

1 ⅜in beading tool
2 1½in roughing gouge
3 ¼in bowl gouge
4 ½in skew chisel

Mount a piece of ½in-thick scrap wood to the faceplate and turn to a smooth disc. With a ⅜in bowl gouge, ▶ make a recess in the centre of this disc to fit the ball on the end of the salt spoon. It will be necessary to chisel a slot in the faceplate running through the central recess in order to permit the work to be mounted more securely.

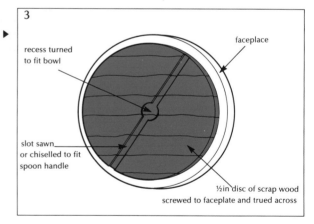

recess turned to fit bowl

faceplace

slot sawn or chiselled to fit spoon handle

½in disc of scrap wood screwed to faceplate and trued across

There are two methods of fitting the work to the ◀ faceplate. In the first, hot-melt glue is applied sparingly to both the arm and the ball. One dab from the glue gun to each of the two points is all that is needed. Check that the work is central in rotation and then hollow out the ball to form the scoop.

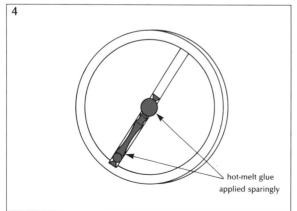

hot-melt glue applied sparingly

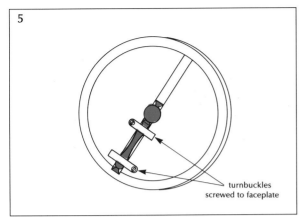

5

turnbuckles
screwed to faceplate

The second method of fitting is to use turnbuckles on the faceplate as shown. These take longer to prepare but are more satisfactory in that the work can be moved as required in order to centre exactly on the faceplate. Once the correct position has been established, hot-melt glue can again be used for added stability.

In hollowing the scoop, do not allow the bottom of the scoop to be over-thick or both the appearance and balance of the scoop will be affected. As in the kitchen scoop, aim for a uniform wall thickness throughout. After the bulk has been removed by a ¼in bowl gouge, a small scraper may be needed to finish the inside shape and wall thickness.

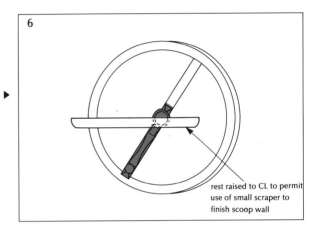

6

rest raised to CL to permit
use of small scraper to
finish scoop wall

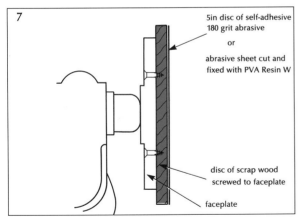

7

5in disc of self-adhesive
180 grit abrasive

or

abrasive sheet cut and
fixed with PVA Resin W

disc of scrap wood
screwed to faceplate

faceplate

Waste can be removed with either a parting tool, a junior hack-saw or, if it is not too bulky, a sanding disc (*see* step 8, page 63). A final coat of sanding sealer is applied and, when dry, is burnished by hand with shavings and coated with a thin coat of Danish oil and allowed to dry.

The sketch shows an alternative pattern of scoop used as a mustard server. This is simpler to make in that the ball at the end of the handle is not hollowed, but is merely sanded flat on both sides using a sanding disc mounted on a faceplate. Finish by hand after sanding, using sanding sealer and Danish oil, and burnishing by hand.

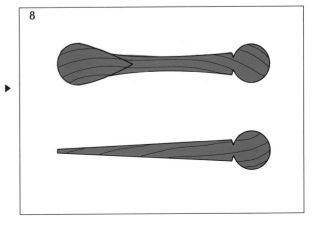

8

This child's spinning top is made from scrap wood but is a particularly good pattern in that it should spin for ▶ approximately two-and-a-half minutes. During this time it can be thrown in the air and caught repeatedly. In addition, the child can use felt-tip pens for colouring it. The blank is made up as shown and is pegged and glued.

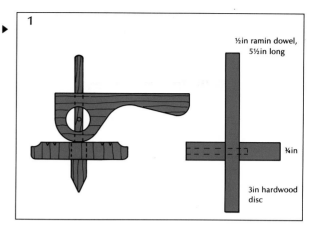

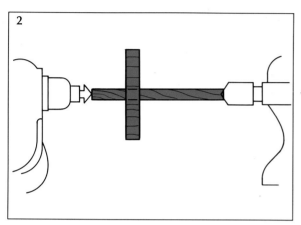

The spinning disc is rounded with a ⅜in bowl gouge to bring it into balance and either a ½in or 1in skew chisel ▶ is then used to ensure that the upper and lower faces of the disc are true. If this is not done thoroughly, the top will not spin steadily and accurately. Should the work catch on the tool, increase tailstock pressure but not too much or the dowel will split.

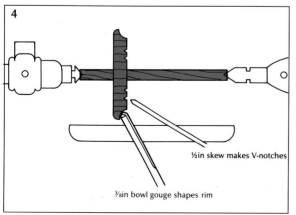

½in skew makes V-notches

⅜in bowl gouge shapes rim

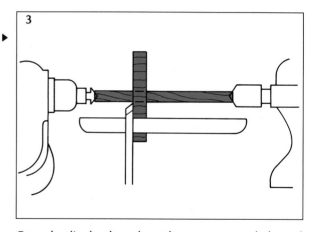

½in ramin dowel, 5½in long

¾in

3in hardwood disc

The blank is mounted on the lathe with the short point ◀ towards the driving head where the two-pronged drive has been replaced by a dead-centre. The reason for this change is that there are two quite different diameters to this top and, if a two-prong or four-prong drive is used on the dowel and an attempt is made to round the spinning disc, the dowel might fracture. By replacing the two-prong drive with a dead-centre, if the work does catch and stop, then the top blank will slip and no damage will be done.

Once the disc has been brought to an accurate balanced ◀ shape, it can be shaped further using either a bowl gouge or a skew chisel on the rim and then sanded and decorated as shown in the illustration.

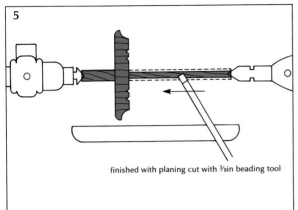

5

finished with planing cut with ⅜in beading tool

The shaft size for the spinning top is ⅜in diameter. The shaft size on the blank is ½in diameter. The surplus is taken off with a ⅜in bowl gouge until near the required diameter and then a flat plate gauge is used to come down precisely to ⅜in using a ⅛in beading tool. The ⅛in beading tool, working as a square chisel, will give a fine flat finish to the upper end of the shaft.

The nose of the spinning top is shaped with a ½in skew chisel as shown, and then the shape from the underside of the disc is brought into balance with the ⅜in beading tool which finally curves the nose and parts it off. It does not matter whether the nose is brought down to any particular size. Finally a hole is drilled for the leather thong.

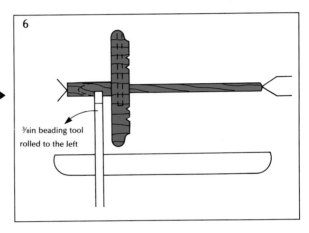

6

⅜in beading tool
rolled to the left

The most convenient way of making the handle is to draw a cardboard template, and from this as many handles as are required can be cut from scrap 1in timber. With the flat upper side reversed, drill a ⁷⁄₁₆in hole to give a good clearance for the ⅜in shaft. Turning the handle on its side, drill with a 1¼in saw-tooth bit to give the central hole. These bits will give a fine finish in the internal cut which will require no further attention.

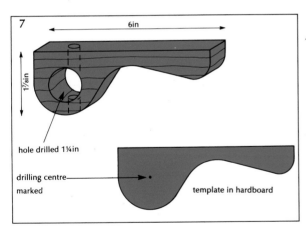

7

6in

1⅞in

hole drilled 1¼in

drilling centre
marked

template in hardboard

The method of operation is to wind a length of leather thong of ¹⁄₁₆in square (a boot-lace) into the hole drilled in the centre of the shaft. A firm pull on the leather thong will spin the top; it will fall free through the handle and spin on any flat surface. Experience has shown that the ideal size for the top is 3in. Less than this and it will not spin for as long as is wanted; more than this and young children will have a problem pulling the string sufficiently firmly.

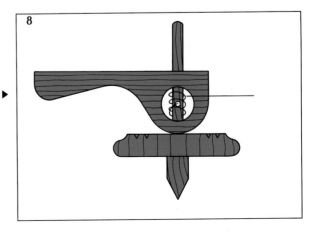

8

In addition to providing a useful cork for a bottle, the exercise is interesting for its use of unconventional tools that the turner should be capable of making for himself. The stopper uses a bought-in optic cork with a ½in central hole. The pattern chosen is that of an acorn, but any pattern can be selected.

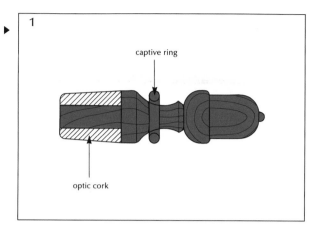

The blank is marked out whilst running the lathe as shown. The use of a dead centre as a driving head is necessary for two reasons. First, any catch with the tool when cutting out the wooden ring will result in a breakage of the ring if a pronged driving centre is used and, second, one needs to use the gauge plate right up to the driving head in order to fit the optic cork bv simple testing and adjustment.

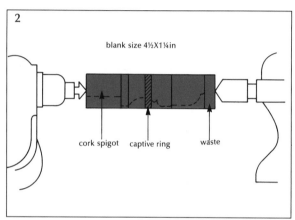

Sufficient room should be allowed on either side of the marked ring to allow the cutting tool to enter. Allow at least ½in waste at the top end of the stopper to prevent the tail centre from splitting the work, since, with a dead-centre drive, the friction has to be increased from time to time to avoid slippage.

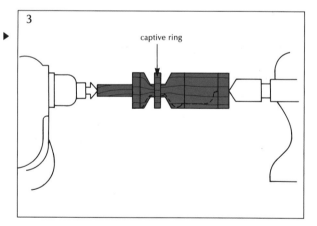

When the slots either side of the ring have been widened, the ring is rounded as far as it can be, and sanded, since as soon as the ring is parted from the body, it will no longer be possible to complete either of these tasks.

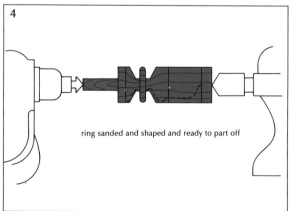

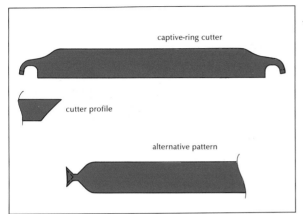

Small tools made by the turner to reproduce special shapes or for special operation are most conveniently made from metal-working files. However, it is not recommended that files be used to make heavy-duty scrapers, since they may fracture. In this exercise, a small tool will be constructed to turn out a wooden ring for the bottle stopper, and it is common sense that in any over-stress the wooden ring would break well before any part of the file. The cutter can be made using either an angle grinder, as in this case, or, it can be made direct from the grinding wheel as shown.

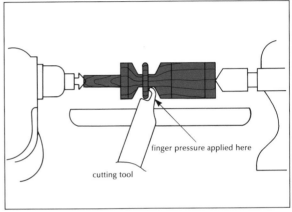

In practice, most of these tools made with file blades are scraping tools and, therefore, the tool is used with the rest raised and the tool itself pointing down. In this case, it is important that pressure is applied behind the cutting point on either side, as there can be no leverage applied with this tool. In addition, it is important to observe very closely where the cutting point is going in order to minimize the residual flashing that will occur just as the ring is parted off.

With the ring running free on the stem, a ¼in bowl gouge can be used to smooth the stem on either side, and a beading tool to produce the small decorative collar below the acorn cup. The head of the acorn is rounded over with a skew chisel and a small pip is left on the end of the acorn before parting off with either a skew chisel or a junior hack-saw.

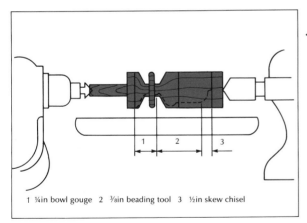

1 ¼in bowl gouge   2 ⅜in beading tool   3 ½in skew chisel

The stopper is mounted in a three-jaw Jacob's chuck and turned for sanding, sealing, burnishing and polishing. Some trial and error may be required in fitting the work to the Jacob's chuck to ensure central running. Finally, with some glue to hold it, the optic cork is slid onto the spigot and the project is complete.

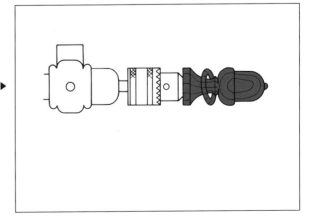

This is a further example of a home-produced form tool being necessary to the turner, since the inside of the thimble must be of a reproducible shape in order that it can fit to a mandrel for final finishing and polishing. If a scroll chuck is used, then the blank requires no preparation and the thimble can be turned directly from the square. In other cases, it is necessary to prepare the blank as shown in order that it can be mounted in a three-jaw Jacob's chuck.

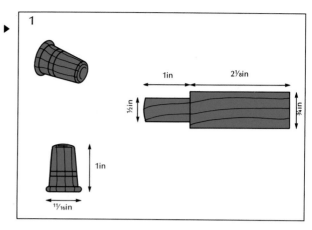

The illustration shows the blank mounted to a Jacob's chuck, and a $\frac{7}{16}$ in No. 1 MT drill bit mounted in the tailstock. These imperial sized tapered bits are readily available from second-hand tool stores and are, at the moment, inexpensive due to the conversion to metric sizes.

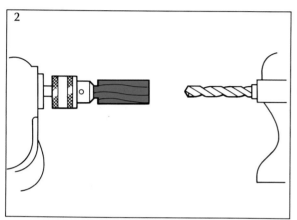

The drill bit is marked with masking tape to show the depth of cut required. The work is run at normal speed and the drill hollows out the bulk of the interior of the thimble. It is not necessary to reduce the speed for this very small operation since the drill bit will not overheat on this small amount of work.

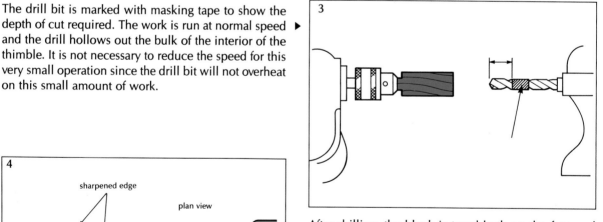

After drilling, the blank is trued both on the face and side as necessary. The form tool for the thimble interior is ground on the coarse grinding wheel to dimensions as shown. Note that the cutting edge is on the forward end and left-hand side only. The rest is set so that the form tool will enter the drilled hole at the centre, and a single horizontal cut is made to form the thimble interior profile.

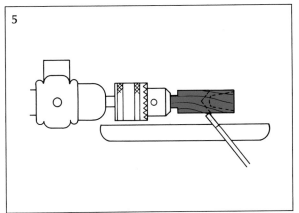

5

The work is set out with the blank running, and a diamond-shaped parting tool is inserted at a 45 degree angle as shown to form the smaller end of the thimble. Take care that the tool enters at the shoulder at 45 degrees and not at the end of the thimble which would result in a badly shaped and elongated product.

The small collar at the larger end of the thimble is formed with a ½in skew chisel and finished with a beading tool. The thimble is then shaped using either a ⅜in bowl gouge, a ⅜in beading tool, or a combination of the two. Decorative lines on the side of the thimble can be added after sanding, and the thimble is parted off using a parting tool before sanding sealer is applied or polishing is complete.

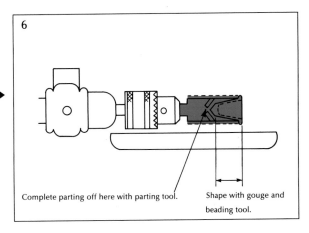

6

Complete parting off here with parting tool.   Shape with gouge and
                                                   beading tool.

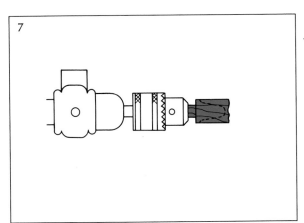

7

With the waste part that is in the chuck after parting off, construct a mandrel as shown so that the thimble is a snug and accurate fit to permit further work on the rings on the face and also polishing to a finish. Care should be taken to ensure that the taper on the mandrel matches the taper inside the thimble, and that the thimble cannot rock. Movement of this kind will damage the work when the rings are incised on the end.

The thimble is mounted on the mandrel and rings are cut on the nose using a ½in skew chisel as shown. Then sanding sealer is applied inside and out and the item is finished in the usual way. Should the thimble show signs of vibrating when the top rings are being cut, this can be cured either by re-shaping the mandrel or by a touch with a hot-melt glue stick to hold the thimble steady.

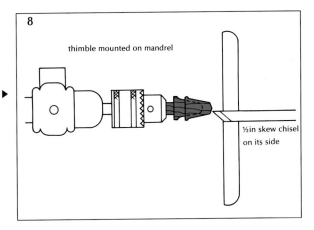

8

thimble mounted on mandrel

½in skew chisel
on its side

This article is typical of the kitchen and general household treen (items made from trees) produced during the Victorian age, frequently from such woods as lignum-vitae and dark stained mahogany. It is a useful exercise in hollow-ware where both the acorn cup and the acorn are arranged to be held separately whilst being hollowed and shaped. Alternative patterns, such as coin holders or small trinket boxes, are shown in addition to the thimble holder.

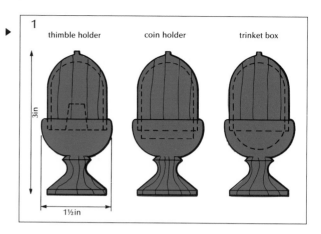

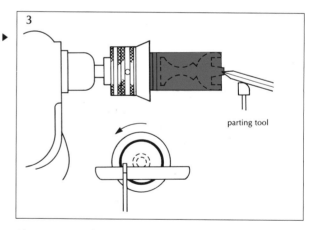

Turn the square blank between centres to a cylinder, trim both ends and prepare for compression holding of either end in a duplex or scroll chuck. Having checked that both ends will fit the duplex chuck chosen (in this case a Masterchuck), set out the work whilst running as shown. Part off the acorn with a parting tool held in the right hand leaving the left hand to catch the acorn on release.

Hollowing the acorn cup will mean turning into end-grain and this will provide the greatest stress; therefore, this operation is done first. The face is marked and then cut to size with a parting tool as shown, and the waste is taken out with the same tool. It is essential that the wall of the acorn cup should be both smooth and vertical to ensure a good sliding fit. After sanding, decorate the thimble upstand in the centre, remove the work from the Masterchuck, and put it on one side.

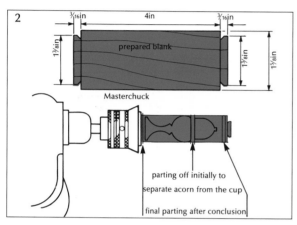

The acorn end is now mounted in the chuck on the spigot prepared in step 2 above, and the centre is hollowed with a ⅜in and a ¼in gouge as shown. Wall thickness is judged by measuring across the maximum diameter of the acorn cup hollow. This will be the eventual outside of the acorn. Subtract ¼in and this will give the inside diameter required.

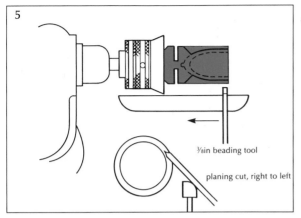

The method of fitting the acorn to the acorn cup is as follows. Calliper the aperture across the acorn cup and then, using a parting tool, come down to this diameter on the exterior of the acorn. Using a ⅜in beading tool, take very fine cuts, making sure that the acorn is both flat and parallel, until the acorn cup is just able to ride onto the acorn. By cutting with the ⅜in beading tool, a fine controlled finish can be achieved.

Complete shaping the outside of the acorn, then sand and finish in the usual way, and part off. Re-mount the acorn cup as shown with the acorn now mounted in it. This will permit final finishing of the top of the acorn and the whole can now be parted through with a parting tool.

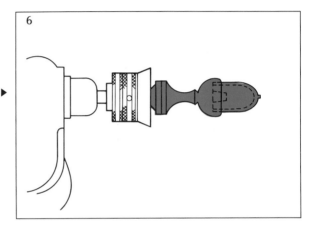

Construction of the alternative patterns is easier than making the thimble holder with the central upstand. The illustration shows dimensioned alternative patterns for a coin holder, and a small jewellery box.

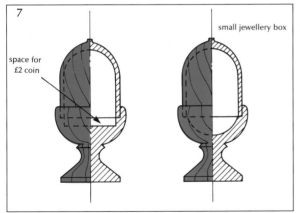

A typical piece of Victorian treen is the kitchen string holder illustrated. This would be the larger alternative to the thimble holder made in this section and would require a heavier base for stability. The construction method is similar.

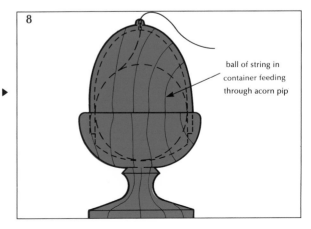

This useful article illustrates the method of reversing face work and finally parting off on the face. Both operations are routinely used in the preparation of clocks and barometer cases.

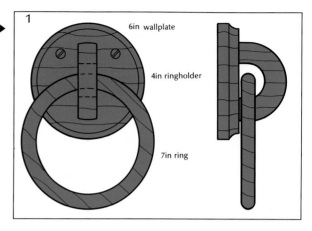

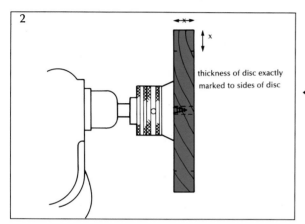

The disc is drilled with a ¼in drill right through to permit mounting to the screw chuck of the Masterchuck. Ideally, both faces should be planed flat, and thicknessed; however, only one face planed flat is acceptable if a thicknesser is not available. The blank is rounded to a true disc and the ring is set out by measuring the thickness of the disc, and then marking a ring on each face the same distance from the rim.

The rim of the disc is rounded using a ⅜in beading tool, treating the disc like a very large bead. This completes two of the quadrants of the ring. The third quadrant is formed by moving the rest to the face of the work and putting a parting tool half-way through the work outside the marked ring. The third quadrant is then turned with a ½in skew chisel and the ⅜in beading tool.

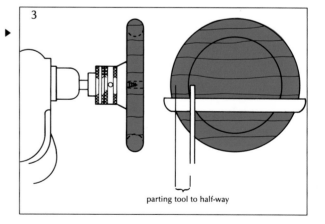

To ensure accurate re-mounting on the reverse side, the centre is slightly dished. The work is sanded and then finished in the usual way, unwound from the chuck and re-mounted on its other face. The fourth quadrant is cut using the parting tool into one-third of the thickness and rounding with the ⅜in beading tool and ½in skew chisel.

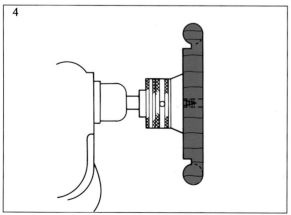

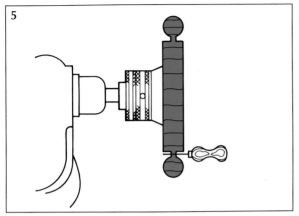

By inserting the point of the bradawl into the slot, the ◄ alignment of the two slots for parting off can be checked, as can the remaining thickness of wood.

Part off with a diamond-shaped parting tool held in the right hand while the left hand lightly holds the rotating ► ring. The ring will stop dead in the hand when it comes free; it has very little residual energy. There will usually be some slight flashing on the inside of the ring which can be removed. You can use a rotating cylinder, carrying an abrasive paper stuck to the outside, run between centres, or the ring can be mounted on a tapered disc and re-cut if there is a sizable step where the parting took place.

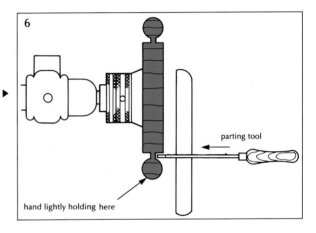

parting tool

hand lightly holding here

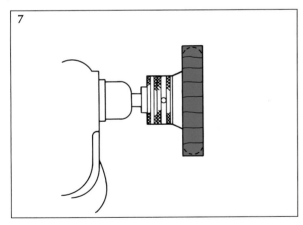

The waste from the centre of the ring can be used to ◄ make the ring holder as shown. On completion it is drilled with a 1¼in saw-tooth bit and cut on the band-saw slightly off-centre to accommodate the ring.

The wall plate is turned, single chucked as shown, holes are drilled for mounting and the towel ring, towel ring ► holder and wall plate are assembled by glueing.

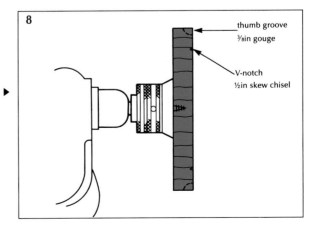

thumb groove
⅜in gouge

V-notch
½in skew chisel

The popular scale for doll's house furniture and fittings is $\frac{1}{12}$ scale. Dolls-house makers frequently require miniature turnings for newel posts, stair bannisters and roof balusters. The illustration shows typical turnings for this purpose. For convenience, these are turned from ramin stripwood which is readily obtainable in square sizes. Frequently, the requirement is for five or six dozen of these small items. For smaller quantities any hardwood thicknessed down to the required square is suitable.

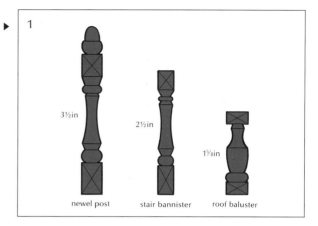

1

3½in — newel post
2½in — stair bannister
1⅜in — roof baluster

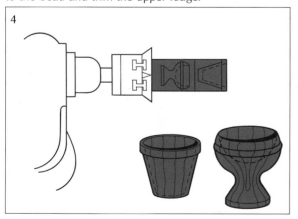

2

sharpened pins set to identify centres

The illustration shows a roof baluster for a doll's 'town house'. In this case, the sequence of work is (1) Place pattern between centres and mark both pummels and centre high point on the masking tape applied to the rest. Replace pattern with blank. (2) Make pummels with ½in skew chisel. (3) Make lower bead with fluted parting tool inserted slowly. (4) With a ¼in bowl gouge, bring remaining section to a round and then hollow the upper section. (5) With a ⅜in beading tool, round down to the bead and trim the upper ledge.

Find accurately the centre on a large number of blanks, a simple jig is constructed as shown. The jig is made from hardwood scrap and it is convenient to allow for centre-finding in two square sizes by fitting a marking spike in either end. In use, the blank is offered up to the correct centre-finder and then tapped with a light hammer to engrave the spike point. Every dozen or so markings, check that the centre-finder is holding correct centre. The point is easily adjusted by bending it to the correct position with a screwdriver.

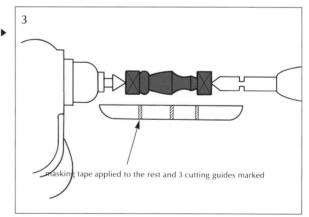

3

masking tape applied to the rest and 3 cutting guides marked

Occasionally, hollowed items such as flower pots and tubs or buckets are required. Mount sufficient material for two items between centres and turn down to required diameter, one end being taken down to 1in diameter to fit the four-jaw self-centring chuck. Complete all hollowing with a ¼in bowl gouge before any shaping of the outside is attempted. The outside is shaped with a ⅜in bowl gouge. Each item is sanded and finished, then parted off with the parting tool.

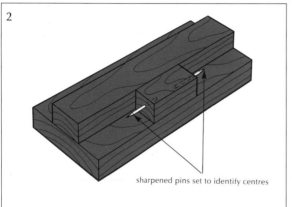

4

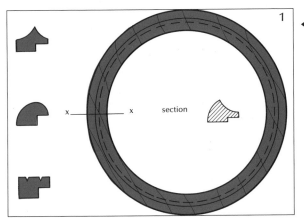

section

The blank is prepared as in step 2, page 74 with a drilled ¼ in hole through the work to suit the Masterchuck. The disc is rounded and set out as shown in the illustration. The hole is through-drilled to facilitate accurate re-centring on the other face.

This is a further example of parting off on the face in face-plate working. It is advisable to have the circular glass prepared beforehand and probably more convenient to have it cut professionally in a variety of sizes to suit the frames that you will make. The illustration shows a selection of profiles, the only common feature being the necessity for a rebate to contain glass, picture or photograph, and backing.

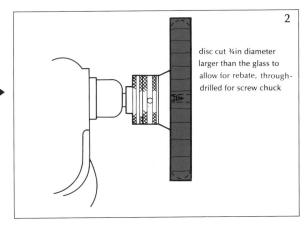

disc cut ¾in diameter larger than the glass to allow for rebate, through-drilled for screw chuck

plan view

centre slightly dished

skew chisel making V-notch

The blank is reversed to form the rebate. A parting tool is used to produce a continuously flat rebate throughout the operation. Parting off is similar in manner to that described in step 5, page 75. There will always be a small amount of flashing to be cut out using a small craft knife. This small cut edge is sanded and finished by hand.

The rest is moved across the face and a parting tool is put half-way through the material. The face of the frame is formed with a beading tool, skew chisel and bowl gouge, depending upon the shape required. At this stage the work is then sanded, decorated if required, and finished with sanding sealer and wax. The waste in the centre is slightly dished for accurate re-mounting.

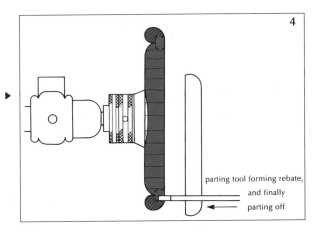

parting tool forming rebate,
and finally
parting off

The egg is an ideal shape for showing the grain, figuring and colouring of various woods, and is a much easier article to make than a ball. They can, of course, be made in various sizes; the suggested size is as shown in the illustration. Do not make the stand too big or it will diminish the impact of the turned egg. ▶

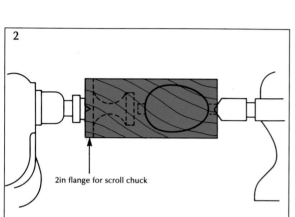

Mount between centres in the normal way, turn to a cylinder and set out both stand and egg as shown. In this case it is intended that a scroll chuck will be used in the latter stage of the turning. ◀

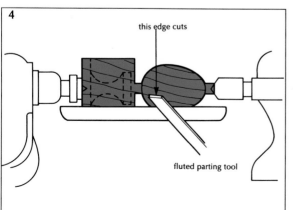

The egg is roughly shaped using a ⅜in bowl gouge and a ½in skew chisel, leaving two ½in diameter spigots on either side. A copy turning stand will be found useful at this stage (*see* step 3, page 85) with a large hen's egg as a model. ▶

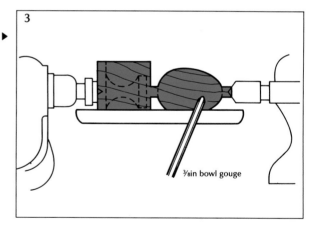

With rough shaping completed, it is possible to use a fluted parting tool to produce long shavings by cutting on its upper edge, as shown. This allows exact adjustment to shape, and by using the point of the fluted parting tool the spigots can be reduced to ¼in diameter on either side. ◀

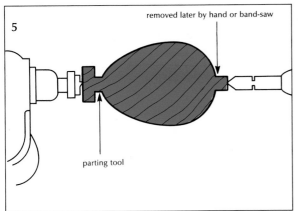

The egg is sanded to its final finish and then finished with sanding sealer and wax. Then the spigots are reduced to ⅛in diameter, and the egg parted off on the end nearest the driving head, the tailstock end being taken off by hand with a hack-saw or a band-saw.

In order to finish both ends of the egg adequately, a hollow jig is made with a ⅜in bowl gouge to support the egg whilst either end is being sanded. It may be necessary to use various layers of tissue paper to ensure a tight fit of the work in the jig.

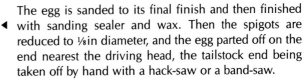

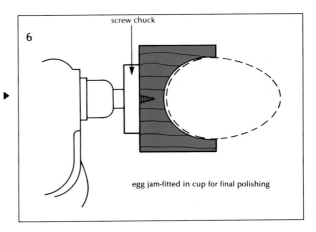

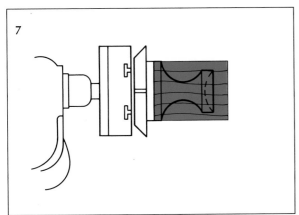

From the waste obtained in the first operation, the stand is turned by mounting in the scroll chuck and turning to shape as shown. An alternative turning technique would be to mount the blank in a scroll chuck in the first place. With care, a finish can be cut and sanded without using a jig.

If you want to make a number of eggs of identical shape, then it will be necessary to construct a template. This will best be produced in hardboard. You may want to turn a bowl to hold these special eggs, ideally each with as much contrasting colour as possible. Display the eggs either singly in a stand, or in a group in a bowl as shown.

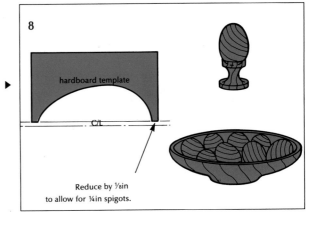

In this example a 3in ball is chosen, but the same principles would apply to turning full-scale skittle balls. As with the egg, it is convenient to have a stand, in this case to prevent the ball rolling about. The 3in ball is prepared from a blank of 3½in width and 5in length, mounted between centres in the usual way.

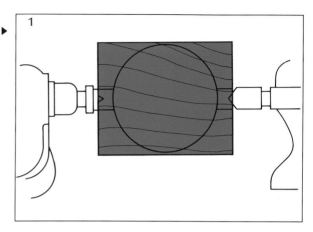

1

Having turned the work to a cylinder, calliper down to 3in diameter along the cylinder length, using a 1½in roughing gouge single-handed, the callipers being held in the left hand. Then set out the blank in pencil as shown using the same callipers to give the distance on the other major axis.

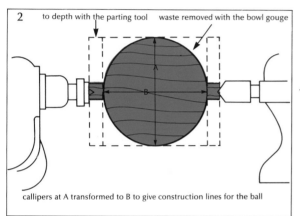

2 to depth with the parting tool   waste removed with the bowl gouge

callipers at A transformed to B to give construction lines for the ball

The left and right spigots are cut with a parting tool at either end of the 3in cylinder and a ⅜in bowl gouge is used to shape the ball roughly. A sighting mask in hardboard is prepared as shown. This is most easily made by pinning the hardboard to a wooden blank mounted on a face-plate, marking the 3in diameter required, and taking out the centre with a skew chisel.

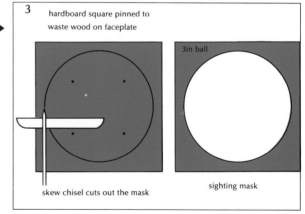

3 hardboard square pinned to
waste wood on faceplate

3in ball

skew chisel cuts out the mask

sighting mask

4

ball view through sighting mask

With the rest removed and the spotlamp centred, the sighting mask is used to view the rotating ball. Inequalities then become apparent and can be marked up in pencil as the ball rotates. The mask is then put aside and a fluted parting tool is used to cut away the excess as shown by the pencil marks. The sighting mask is backed up by use of callipers across not only the major and minor axes, but also across the diagonals. Material is removed as necessary.

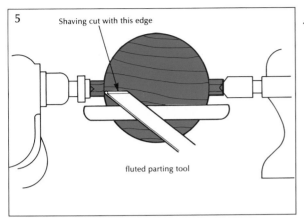

The whole of the ball is then sanded, it is finished and polished, and parted off leaving the minimum amount of spigot at either end. The stand is turned to the pattern as shown.

A bowl of smaller diameter rim than 3in can be used as an additional check. Since the bowl rim is turned circular, any inequalities in the ball will show up as the bowl is put to the rotating work. Mark as before with pencil and take off the excess material with the top edge of the fluted parting tool as illustrated.

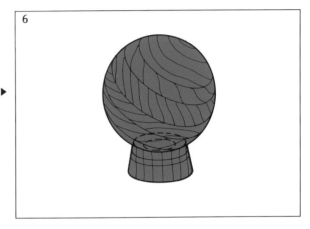

A hollow jig is turned with a ⅜in bowl gouge to fit the 3in ball; this fitting is accomplished by trial and error and, if necessary, by backing with tissue to ensure a snug fit. It is not advisable to attempt to sand the other axis of the ball; it is best to use the jig to smooth and finish the two parted ends as turned between centres. These can then be given a coat of sanding sealer and finished with wax in the normal manner.

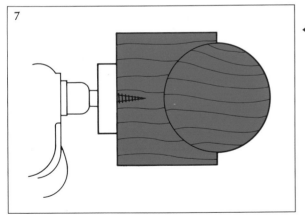

Although not strictly woodturning in the true sense of the word, balls of any size can be turned using a router and gimbal cage. The illustration shows how this is done leaving only the smallest spigot at either side of the ball to be finished by hand later.

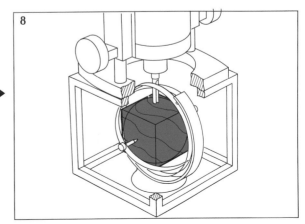

This is a relatively rapid way of making small balls of up to 1½in diameter. Prepare a 1¾in square of material to ▶ form a blank for the ball, setting it out as in step 2, page 80.

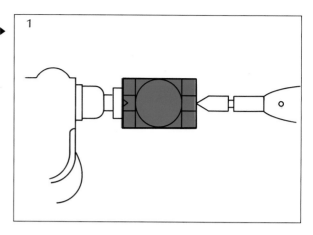

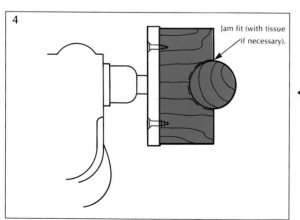

Roughly turn the ball to shape using a ⅜in bowl gouge. ◀ The pipe should be sharpened all round on the coarse grinding wheel to give a sharp hollow bevel, and all-round cutting edge.

The effectiveness of this method depends on the bulk of the work having been previously done with the ⅜in ▶ bowl gouge. The sharpened pipe is used in a swinging action until the ball is round. This method gives an accurate ball. The pipe is only used as a finishing treatment to produce a perfect sphere.

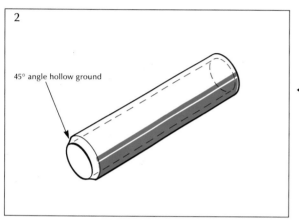

Entire diameter of sharpened pipe is in contact.

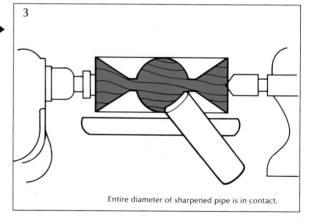

Part off and finish the ball as explained on page 81 using ◀ a suitable jig. These balls, if made in softwood, can be stored in glass jars or closed plastic bags with a few drops of aromatic oil. The balls will absorb the perfume and can then be scattered in drawers among clothes to impart a pleasant perfume to the clothing.

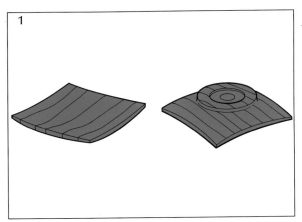

In contrast to conventional bowl turning, the blank is left square and not band-sawed out to a disc. It is important that the square be an accurate square and that the centre is found by the careful construction of diagonal lines. The bowl will be turned by a double chucking system using double-sided tape initially, then double chucking with the scroll chuck to hollow out the best face of the bowl.

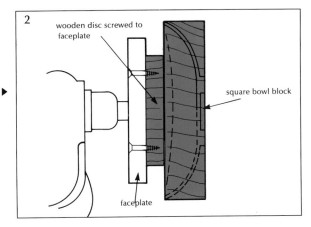

Mount the carefully squared blank to the faceplate containing a scrap wooden disc and double-sided tape, making sure that both faces are flat and dust free. Allow five minutes of clamping, either between headstock and tailstock, vice on the workbench, in a pillar drill, or using any suitable clamp. The rim of the bowl will appear as a moving blur due to the square corners and, at all times from now on, care must be taken to keep fingers and tools well away from this moving blur except when making a calculated cut.

Move the rest to the face and produce a recess for the duplex chuck ¼in in depth. A ⅜in bowl gouge should be used to shape the outside without change of speed or angle as the gaps are encountered. Since this face cannot be sanded with the work moving, care must be taken to ensure a smooth finish with the gouge.

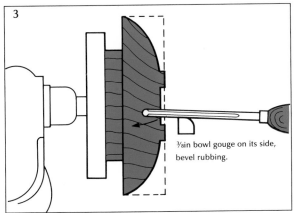

Finishing cuts on the curved surface should be completed with the ⅜in bowl gouge. Reverse the bowl and mount in the duplex chuck. Hollow the face with the bowl gouge. Sand all square corners whilst stationary. Sand the remainder rotating but keep the hands well away from the square corners. Finish with sanding sealer and wax in the usual way.

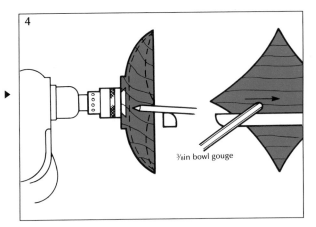

The bowl is turned with either a pin chuck or a large-diameter screw chuck. Choose material which has the bark firmly adhering to the sapwood, otherwise the bark edge will be lost during turning. This can be remedied by glueing the bark edge back on the bowl, but this would cause a delay in turning. Band-saw round cardboard template, then drill out bark face with a 1in bit to accept pin chuck. ▶

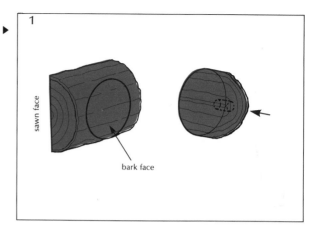

Turn the outside of the bowl in the conventional manner ◀ with a ⅜in bowl gouge, working to the outside, having made a recess to suit either of the duplex chucks. Take care that the rim around the recess is slightly dished in by a fraction. This will avoid the bowl rocking when placed on a flat surface.

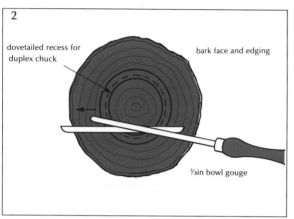

The bowl is removed from the pin chuck. It is re-mounted in the duplex chuck and is hollowed using the ⅜in gouge, taking normal cuts and care when handling ▶ rotating work due to the rough waney edge of the bowl. A conventional depth gauge is not possible with the uneven lip, so a length of dowel with a masking tape marker is used.

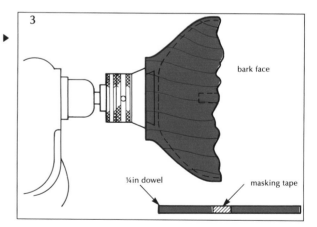

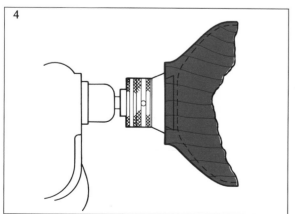

Wall thickness can be checked with the bowl stationary ◀ using finger and thumb. When sufficiently thin and even throughout, the bowl can be sanded provided care is taken when the sandpaper and hand are near the rough lip. The bowl is finished normally with sanding sealer and wax, the sanding sealer covering the bark lip as well as the turned wooden area.

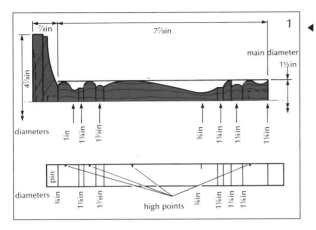

1

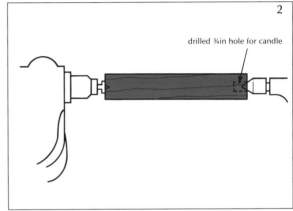

Following the principles explained on page 28, the squared stock is drilled for the candle recess whilst still in the square so that the turning can be completed around the hole. It is usual to allow a ¾in diameter hole for the candle, and this will fit conveniently into the running tail of the tailcentre. Driving with a conventional two-prong drive, turn the remainder of the work to a cylinder and set out with the pattern stick.

Georgian pattern candlesticks (steps 1–8) Good copy turning comes from constant practice and the use of a pattern stick and callipers. The completed candlestick is shown in the illustration with its own pattern stick. Note that the pattern stick should be kept simple – do not mark every change of shape, but only those that are of major importance. Marking every point will lead to confusion when set out on the rotating blank. Similarly it is convenient, at least to start with, to use just one set of callipers and pick off the required dimensions from the pattern as they are needed.

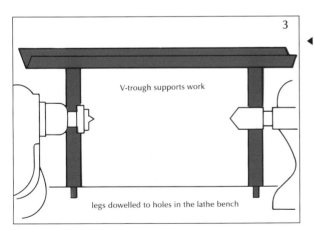

3

The illustration shows the tools required and the direction in which they are moved in order to shape the candlestick down to the predetermined diameters as obtained in the previous step.

A useful workshop-made rig is the copying rest as illustrated, which allows the pattern to be exactly in line behind the rotating work and at a convenient level for the turner. Work methodically from one end to the other, callipering down with callipers and a parting tool to the diameters noted on the pattern stick.

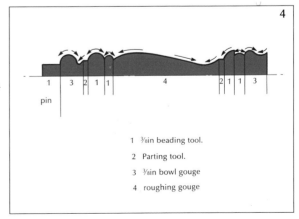

4

1 ⅜in beading tool.

2 Parting tool.

3 ⅜in bowl gouge

4 roughing gouge

Shape curves by eye, and use the gauge plate to turn pins that will fix the standard into the base. For close comparison, remove the work from the lathe and place it on a bench together with the pattern. This will provide a more searching contrast than using the copying rest at a distance. Examine the work for differences, as shown. Also, look for incorrect profiling and diameter. Remount in the lathe and adjust as necessary, finally sanding and finishing in the usual manner.

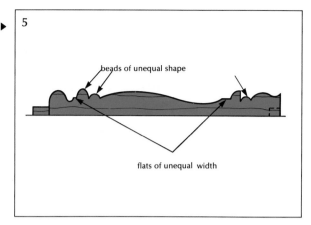

5

beads of unequal shape

flats of unequal width

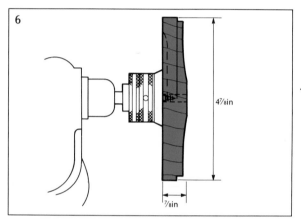

6

4⁷⁄₈in

⁷⁄₈in

The base is drilled with a ¾in saw-tooth bit to fit the stick. It is usual to drill the hole right through. This will remove the evidence of the mounting by the screw chuck.

The base is conveniently turned on a screw chuck which allows the base to be reversed so that both faces can be shaped. A ⁵⁄₁₆ screw chuck inserted in the Masterchuck is a convenient chuck for this purpose, a ¼in hole being drilled right through the work at the beginning. The diameter of the base is taken with a pair of callipers as a ⅜in bowl gouge brings the disc down to size. Reverse the base and hollow out underneath. Sand and finish in the usual manner.

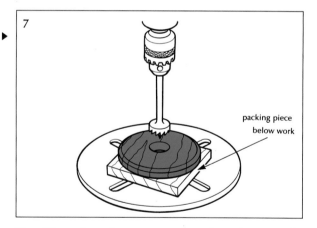

7

packing piece below work

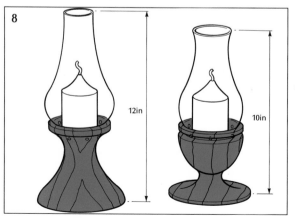

8

12in

10in

The illustration shows examples of modern candle lamps, using a turned wooden base and glass chimney. These usually take a wide candle of 2in diameter, relatively short. In all cases it is necessary to allow for a passage of air up the inside of the glass chimney by drilling holes around the inside. Failure to do this means that the candle will melt to fill out the whole of the bottom of the chimney.

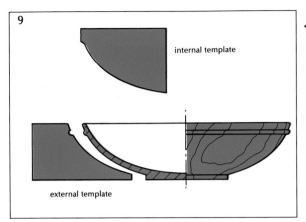

9

internal template

external template

Bowls (steps 9–12) To make exact copies of a bowl, it is necessary to make internal and external templates of the original. The illustration shows these templates. Callipers will also be required to ensure that the rim diameter does not vary.

The required number of bowl blanks should be cut to the same marked diameter on the band-saw and from the same thickness of material. These are then rounded down to a disc and brought down to the exact callipered size required.

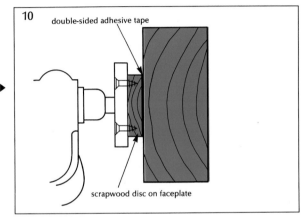

10

double-sided adhesive tape

scrapwood disc on faceplate

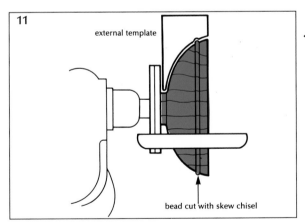

11

external template

bead cut with skew chisel

The bowls can be either double or single chucked. In this case, the example shows a single-chucked bowl, mounted on a faceplate with a wooden disc and double-sided tape. The bowl exterior is shaped first and the template offered up with the work stationary. In use, both the internal and external templates will wear and, after some time, will no longer be accurate. Measuring with the work stationary will prolong their useful lives.

The inside is turned towards the centre with a ⅜in bowl gouge and, constantly checking with the internal template with the work stationary, an exact copy will be produced. Sanding sealer, wire wool and burnishing with shavings, followed by either Briwax or Carnauba wax as a stick, will give the required finish.

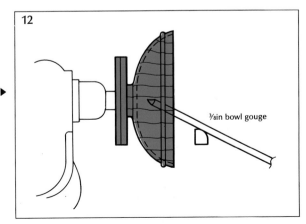

12

⅜in bowl gouge

The Windsor stool (steps 13–20) The illustration shows a finished stool, the required pattern sticks and the router bit used for the moulding underneath the stool seat. The unusual pattern of the stool top is best obtained by using a cardboard template. It should be noted at this stage that the compound angle holes for the stool legs are drilled when the stool seat is still in its rectangular form. This will give improved accuracy.

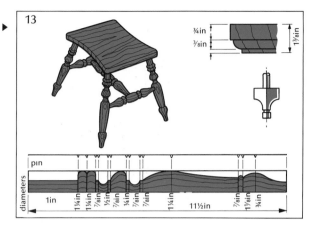

13

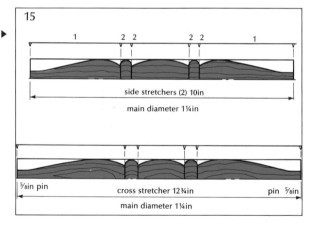

Details of the leg and the pattern stick are shown. Note that the pattern stick is notched for accurate pencil marking. The illustration is numbered to show the type of tool used and the direction in which it is moved: 1½in roughing gouge (1); ⅜in bowl gouge (2); and ⅜in beading tool (3). Reference to page 85 will show the techniques of copy turning employed in producing these four legs.

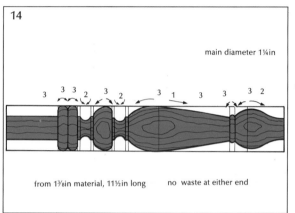

14

main diameter 1¼in

from 1⅜in material, 11½in long   no waste at either end

Side and cross stretchers with their own pattern sticks are shown. Tools used are shown numbered on the illustration: 1½in roughing gouge (1); ⅜in beading tool (2). The usual copy turning techniques are followed; that is to say callipering first to diameter, having marked the break points, and then rounding down by comparison using the copy turning stand.

15

side stretchers (2) 10in
main diameter 1¼in

⅝in pin   cross stretcher 12¾in   pin ⅝in
main diameter 1¼in

The stool seat can be drilled using a saw-tooth bit in a pillar drill with the plate angled to suit. Alternatively, it can be clamped to the workbench, a sliding bevel put alongside the drill (which will be fitted with a flat bit), lines drawn diagonally from leg sockets to leg sockets, and the hole drilled by eye. Although this may appear to be a crude method it is well tried and accurate.

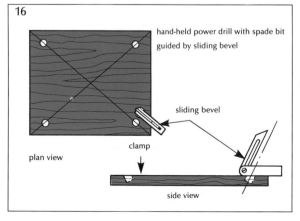

16

hand-held power drill with spade bit guided by sliding bevel

sliding bevel

clamp

plan view

side view

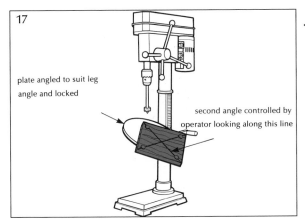

17

plate angled to suit leg
angle and locked

second angle controlled by
operator looking along this line

The seat can now be band-sawed to shape, fixed to the workbench with double-sided tape and then routed on the underside to the required moulding. The hand-held router is guided by the cutter pin, and will require two or three passes.

By drilling with a pillar drill, a saw-tooth bit can be used which means that the leg can be inserted farther into the seat. This will obviously add to strength and stability. Again, the diagonal lines joining the leg holes are used as a guide, the other angle being obtained directly from the angle of the plate of the pillar drill.

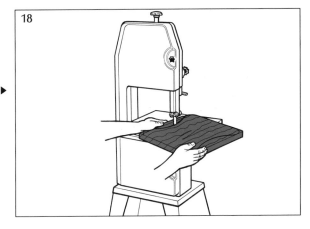

18

Assembly begins by putting cross-stretchers to side-stretchers, legs into side-stretchers and then legs into stool seat. After a check trial assembly the stool can be glued and malletted home.

19

Alternative seat shapes are shown, along with a connected fireside seat which can be dismantled to form individual stools if required. It may be of interest that in one old illustration of a Windsor stool, the legs were referred to as 'Lancashire Pattern'.

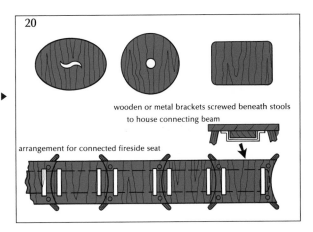

20

wooden or metal brackets screwed beneath stools
to house connecting beam

arrangement for connected fireside seat

The illustration shows a finished chair patterned from a kindergarten chair in use at the end of the nineteenth century. A cutting list for all components follows: backrest: 13¼in×2in×1in thick, but allow 2½in for the curvature; spindles: 8½in (2), 8¼in (2), and 8 from 1in sq.; seat: 11×9½in (depth)×1in; legs: 8¼in from 1⅛in sq.; side stretchers: 8¾in from 1in sq.; cross stretcher: 8½in from ¾in sq. Cardboard templates will be needed for the backrest and the chair seat in addition to the pattern sticks and callipers normally required for copy turning.

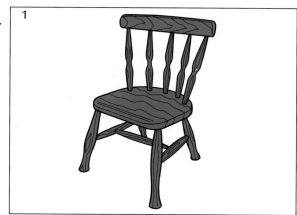

The backrest is marked from a template to 2½in-thick material and then band-sawed out to shape. A belt sander will be found useful for finishing after sawing. The choice of wood is a matter for personal preference. Traditionally, seats are made of elm, and legs of ash, although my own choice is to use one type of wood throughout. English oak is attractive and has adequate strength.

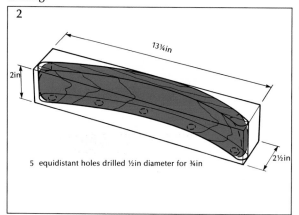

5 equidistant holes drilled ½in diameter for ¾in

The seat is band-sawed to the shape marked by the template and holes drilled as shown in the illustration. The seat is not hollowed in the conventional manner, as a bow or smoker's chair seat would normally be. Drilling the holes in the seat for the legs is best done using a sliding bevel and power drill, following the splay lines shown in the illustration. The holes for the back rest should be drilled after the spindles have been turned, when the angles of the spindles to the seat can be easily seen.

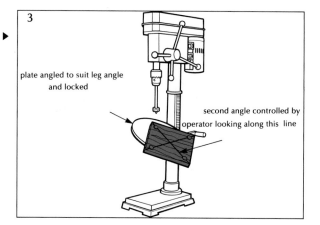

plate angled to suit leg angle and locked

second angle controlled by operator looking along this line

Back spindles are turned using the normal copy turning methods. The illustration is numbered to show the tools and the direction of their movement. The tools should be used in the following sequence: rough to cylinder with roughing gouge; gauge diameter at ends; roughing gouge to centre to form hollow (1–2); roughing gouge to ends to form curve to pin (3–4). Do not allow any waste at either end of the spindle because it is necessary to check the diameters of each with a test block, as shown in step 5, page 91.

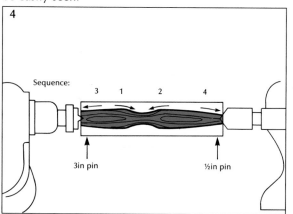

Sequence:

3in pin   ½in pin

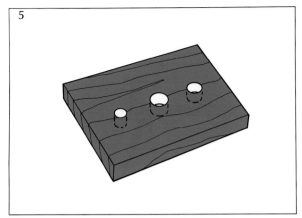

The chair legs are turned in the same manner from 1¼in-square material. Do not allow any waste on either end. The legs end in ¾in pins where they are fitted into the stool seat, and these are dimensioned using the plate gauge. Construct a wooden test block so that stretchers, legs and back spindles can be tested for correct fit before being removed from the lathe.

Side- and cross-stretchers are turned from 1in material in the same manner described in step 5 above. Pins and sockets are ½in diameter. Sockets in the side-stretcher are angled.

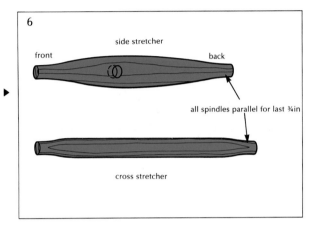
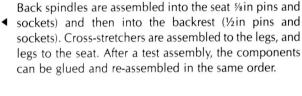

Back spindles are assembled into the seat ⅝in pins and sockets) and then into the backrest (½in pins and sockets). Cross-stretchers are assembled to the legs, and legs to the seat. After a test assembly, the components can be glued and re-assembled in the same order.

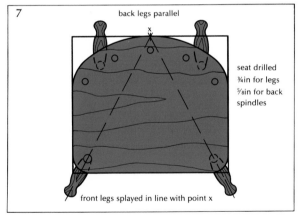

If a shaped seat bottom is required, this can done with an inshave or an Arbotec wheel mounted on an angle-grinder. (The original kindergarten patterns did not have this refinement.)

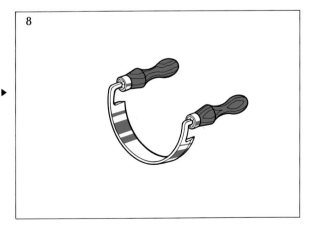

The illustration shows a general view of a Victorian cotton reel holder in use, with dimensions of the various parts. The holder can be made from any decorative wood but looks best in a dark material. Walnut is ideal. The original was turned in mahogany and stained dark.

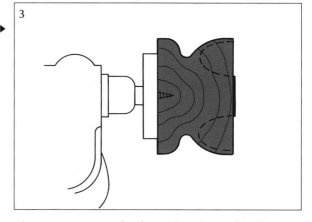

1

pin: 3½in (including ball of ⅝in diameter)

platforms: 4½in diameter ⅜in thick

base: 4½in diameter 3½in high
(may be in 2 pieces if required)

top knot 2in high 1in diameter

top column: 2in high 1¼in diameter

bottom: 2in high 1½in diameter

Drilling the base and column is completed either on a lathe or in a pillar drill whilst the parts are in square. The parts are then turned around the hole to ensure concentricity. A central dowel will join all parts together in the final assembly. The platforms are turned on a screw chuck and drilled after finishing.

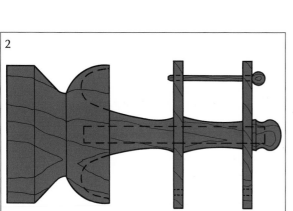

2

The base is turned from a solid to provide a convenient drop for pins and buttons, etc. The two platforms are face-turned using a screw chuck and the pins are turned between centres and parted off in the normal way. Use ½in dowel for the centre column and drill accordingly. Use ¼in holes in the top platform for the removable pins.

3

Alternative patterns for these Victorian reel holders are shown. They are most conveniently made in the various parts shown in step 1 above, but the original, as seen by the author, was turned out of one solid piece, the pins turned and inserted later.

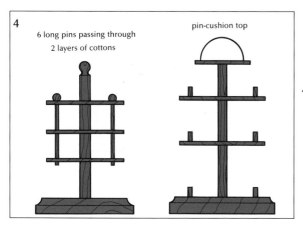

4

6 long pins passing through
2 layers of cottons

pin-cushion top

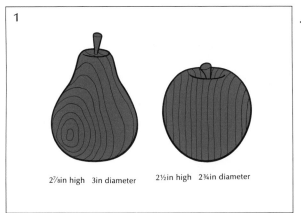

1

2⅞in high   3in diameter   2½in high   2¾in diameter

The illustration gives a general view and dimensions. The blank is prepared for the Masterchuck in compression with one spigot. Both items are turned from the one blank. They can be made from any material. The rounded shapes of the wooden fruit display the piece well. For this reason, exotics are frequently used, and often the apple is made from that wood.

The apple is turned first, using a skew chisel and a ⅜in bowl gouge. Note the angle of parting off the apple to give a dished underside. The stalk for the apple is made separately by turning or carving. A hole is drilled in the top of the apple and the stalk inserted.

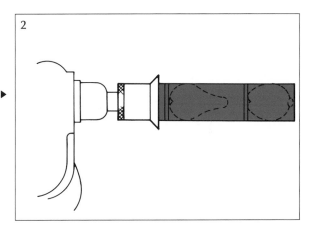

2

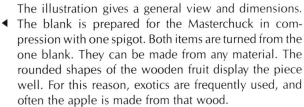

3

base of pear is not dished

The pear follows from the same piece of material, and is turned in a similar manner, together with its stalk. Both items are finished by sanding, sanding sealer, wire wool, burnishing, and wax in the normal way before parting off.

An attractive small jewellery or trinket box can be made from an apple pattern by hollowing the apple. In this case, the blank needs to be prepared with two spigots for use in compression and the technique of hollow-ware turning is exactly the same as in the production of the thimble holder on pages 72 and 73.

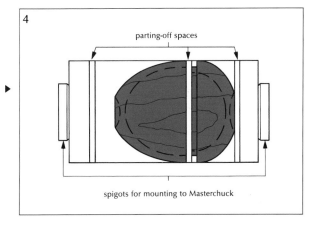

4

parting-off spaces

spigots for mounting to Masterchuck

The convenient chuck for this work is the four-jaw self-centering scroll chuck due to its very strong grip in compression and its ability to tolerate up to 10in unsupported overhang. The illustration gives a general view and the dimensions of the finished vase.

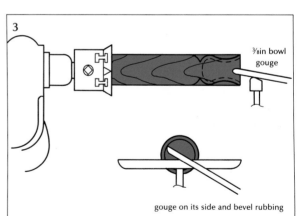

The sequence of turning this vase is important, particularly if a thin stem is required. 1. Hollow bowl with ⅜in gouge and ½in scraper. 2. Shape outside of bowl with gouge and chisel. 3. Sand and finish bowl completely. 4. Bring stem to shape with ⅜in gouge and chisel. 5. Use ⅜in beading tool for ball and ball and diamonds (A). Choose a close-grained wood for strength – holly or hornbeam would be suitable.

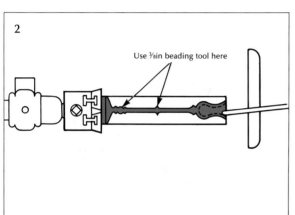

Use ⅜in beading tool here

The bowl of the vase is hollowed and shaped first. If a thin-stemmed vase is required; it should be sanded and completely finished and waxed at this stage. In turning a thin-stemmed vase, any attempt to work on the bowl after the stem has been brought to thinness will be very difficult. The turner should aim to work in sequence from the vase bowl back to the vase foot.

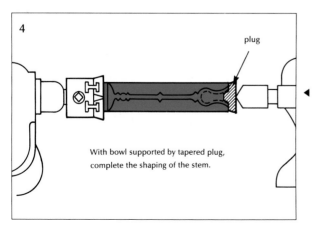

⅜in bowl gouge

gouge on its side and bevel rubbing

A plug is now fitted to the bowl of the vase and supported in the tailstock, so that a thin stem can be tuned and then the base. Note that if a lid is required for the vase, this could be turned using the techniques explained on pages 72 and 73.

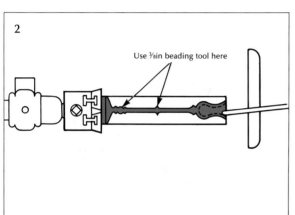

plug

With bowl supported by tapered plug, complete the shaping of the stem.

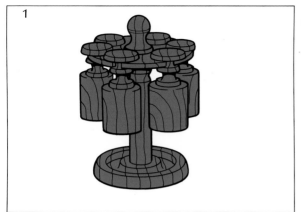

The illustration shows a set of six goblets suspended from a pillar stand which is a more convenient way of storing and displaying the goblets than a wooden box. The goblets are best turned in sycamore or pine and, if they are required to be used for drinking, the finish should be three coats of polyurethane varnish sanded down with wire wool between each coat. A full-scale pattern stick cut from hardboard or cardboard should be made for the central column and the goblets.

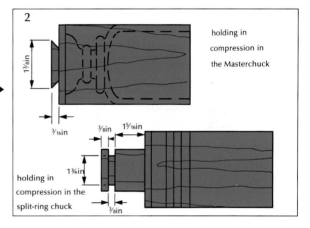

The work is best held in a duplex or a scroll chuck. A screw chuck must not be used, since the holding in end-grain will not be strong enough to permit hollowing out the goblet. The illustration shows the blank prepared for holding in the Masterchuck and also in a six-in-one chuck which is an early form of the modern combination chuck. The work is brought to a cylinder between centres, the tailstock removed, and the work set out, hollowing the bowl of the goblet with a ⅜in bowl gouge. A depth gauge is useful (*see* step 18, page 46).

The goblet stand is turned between centres with the aid of the pattern stick. A ⅝in pin is turned on the top and bottom end to fit the upper and lower discs, most of the work being done with the large roughing gouge and a 1in skew chisel. The hanging plate is drilled to accept the screw chuck and trued to a disc, sanded and decorated. Holes of 1¼in are drilled to hold the goblets, as well as a ⅝in hole to accept the dowelled top finial. The large drilled holes are then sawn out to the perimeter of the disc.

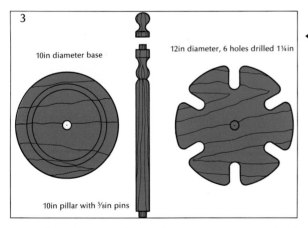

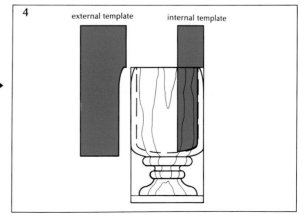

Internal and external templates are constructed of hardboard from the initial goblet and the other five goblets follow the same technique as the first except for the additional work with the templates to ensure that they are all identical. Note that for comfort in use, the lip of each goblet must be brought to a fine point.

First method (steps 1–4) Any hardwood will be suitable for these items. Alternatively, yew gives a high polish and a pleasant appearance. Turn the blank between the centres to a 2in diameter, true both ends with a skew chisel, place in a pillar drill and drill with a saw-tooth bit of 1¼in diameter. Use a drilling vice for this operation and drill from both ends of the blank. ▶

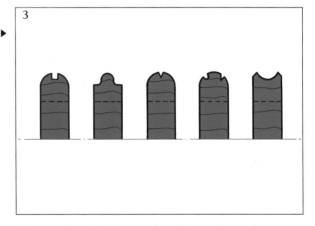

Holding the rounded work very securely, band-saw the work into hoops, slightly oversized, on the finished napkin ring. From softwood make a mandrel with a slow taper from 1⅜in diameter down to 1⅛in. The hoops are singly jam-fitted onto this mandrel. The mandrel should be 8in long and driven between centres by a two-prong driving head. ◀

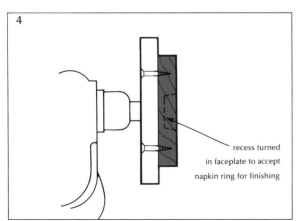

1⅜in 1⅛in

8in

tapered mandrel in softwood

With the blank on the tapered mandrel, true both ends and turn the exterior of the ring. Each ring will normally be different from the others in the set in order that the user can recognize his own napkin ring. The illustration shows a variety of turned patterns for these rings. ▶

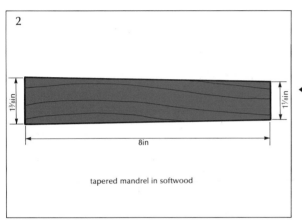

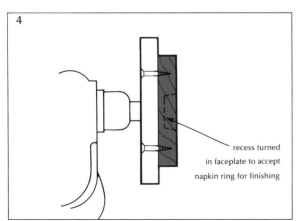

recess turned
in faceplate to accept
napkin ring for finishing

Mount scrap wood onto a faceplate and turn the recess, which will be a jam fit, for the napkin ring. A little trial and error will show what taper is required for this purpose. The ring can now be finished on the inside to provide an easy sliding entrance for the napkin. It can also be finished and polished. ◀

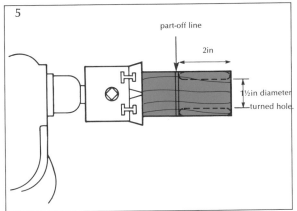

Set out the 1½in diameter on the face and take out material to depth using a ⅜in and a ¼in bowl gouge. When the bulk of the material has been removed, true the inside of the cylinder with a 1in skew chisel, finish shaping the rounded edge of the ring, sand and finish as much of the ring as is showing, and part off from the chuck.

Second method (steps 5–8) In this case the napkin ring is turned from the side using a scroll chuck, without drilling. The square blank is mounted in a four-jaw self-centring chuck and turned to a cylinder. This is a larger napkin ring than the one turned in the first method, and the inside hole will be 1½in diameter.

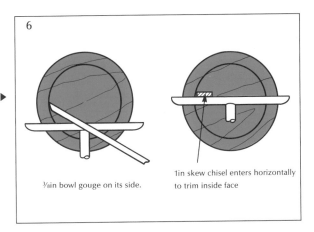

Re-mount the ring in the scroll chuck, true the interior and exterior, and shape the outer face of the napkin ring. Sand and finish and unload the ring from the chuck. Care should be taken, when clamping up in this last operation, that not too much pressure is put on the chuck jaws or the ring may be marked.

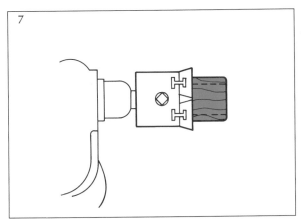

Various patterns of napkin ring decoration are shown. In addition, inlays in silverware, contrasting woods and black friction lines produced by the use of stainless steel wire running in a nick on the exterior, provide plenty of options. A pyrography machine, used either free-hand or with alphabet heads, can be used to name napkin rings.

The illustration shows the general arrangement of the tapestry frame and dimensions to suit a tapestry width of 22in. The screw threading is best produced in sycamore or beech, but the remainder of the frame can be in any hardwood – oak, mahogany or sweet chestnut all being ideal.

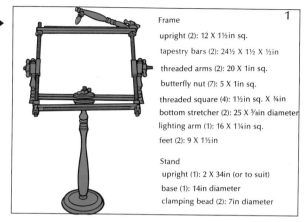

Frame

upright (2): 12 X 1½in sq.

tapestry bars (2): 24½ X 1½ X ½in

threaded arms (2): 20 X 1in sq.

butterfly nut (7): 5 X 1in sq.

threaded square (4): 1½in sq. X ¾in
bottom stretcher (2): 25 X ⅝in diameter
lighting arm (1): 16 X 1¼in sq.

feet (2): 9 X 1½in

Stand

upright (1): 2 X 34in (or to suit)

base (1): 14in diameter

clamping bead (2): 7in diameter

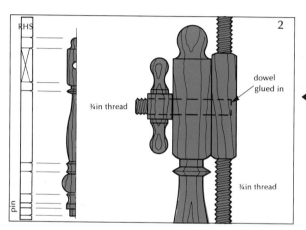

dowel glued in

¾in thread

¾in thread

The pattern stick for the upright is shown. Note that the frame must be able to swing right over in reverse in order to allow the tapestry-maker to work on the back of the tapestry canvas. An exploded view shows the arrangements for tightening at the pivot of the frame with the upright.

The tapestry bars are simple laths drilled at either end with a ¾in saw-tooth bit to allow the screw threading to run through them. The pattern for the stretcher base is shown. This allows the tapestry frame to be used in three ways – from an armchair, on a table, or free-standing on a stand.

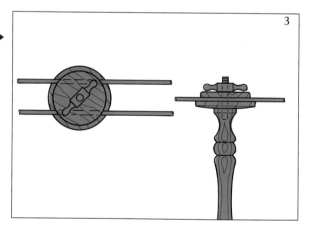

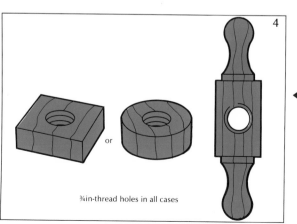

or

¾in-thread holes in all cases

The wood screw threading is produced using a ¾in screw box, having turned the dowel to size and tapered and waxed it as explained on page 32. The round, square, and butterfly nuts are produced by drilling a pilot hole and threading with the tap, again as explained on page 32. The threaded, circular, or square nuts are used internally to tension the tapestry; the larger butterfly nuts are used externally to hold the frame to the mounting and the mounting to the stand.

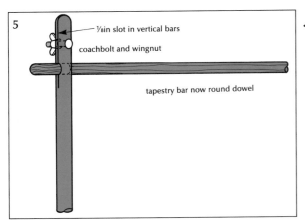

5
1/8in slot in vertical bars
coachbolt and wingnut
tapestry bar now round dowel

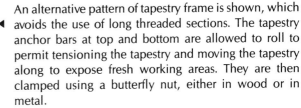

An alternative pattern of tapestry frame is shown, which avoids the use of long threaded sections. The tapestry anchor bars at top and bottom are allowed to roll to permit tensioning the tapestry and moving the tapestry along to expose fresh working areas. They are then clamped using a butterfly nut, either in wood or in metal.

The pattern of the stand is optional provided that the height of the tapestry frame is comfortable for the tapestry-maker when seated in a chair of the height and pattern that he will use when working at the frame. The method of fixing the tapestry frame to the stand is shown in the exploded detail in step 3, page 98.

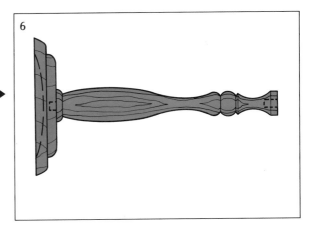

6

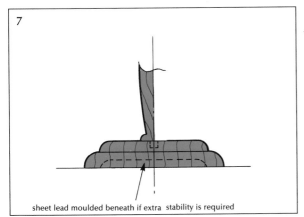

7

sheet lead moulded beneath if extra stability is required

The detail for the base is illustrated. Again, the pattern is optional provided that the base is sufficiently heavy to provide stability. If extra stability is needed, dish the base by ¼in and inlay a disc of sheet lead obtainable from a builder. The lead can be held in place with ½in countersunk screws.

In both patterns the tapestry must be firmly fixed to the anchoring bars, and this is best achieved by either stapling the tapestry along the length of the bar and then adding a carpet tack every three inches, or putting a continuous strip of adhesive from a hot-melt glue gun and pressing the tapestry onto the glue, again reinforcing it with upholstery tacks every three inches.

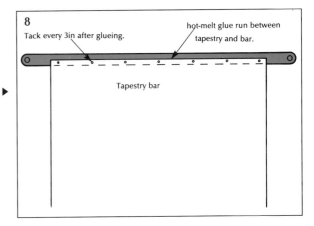

8
Tack every 3in after glueing.
hot-melt glue run between tapestry and bar.
Tapestry bar

Salt and pepper mill mechanisms come in various sizes from 6in to 18in. The illustration shows the pattern for a 14in mill. Saw-tooth bits are the more convenient pattern for the drilling required, but flat bits will be found to be adequate. Sycamore, beech and elm are popular woods for these items. In order to obtain a good joint and grain match between the body and the cap, it is important to follow the sequence precisely.

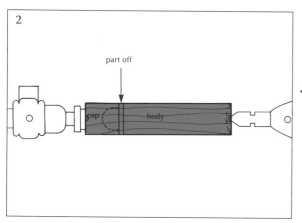

With a two-pronged centre, mount the work between centres, round to a cylinder with a roughing gouge, and set out the work with a pencil. Then square the cap end (nearest the driving head), slightly dish the bottom of the mill (nearest the tailstock) and part the cap from the body either with a hack-saw or by taking the work to a band-saw.

Put the cap on one side, and place the body between centres with the body base facing the tailstock and the body held at the headstock end in a scroll chuck in compression. A Jacob's chuck is mounted in the tailstock with a 1¼in saw-tooth bit. Drill in for ½in, replace the saw-tooth bit with a 1in bit, and drill to just over half-way down the body.

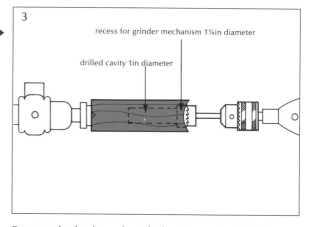

Reverse the body and, with the 1in saw-tooth bit, complete drilling through to meet the hole previously made. If a scroll chuck is not available, this drilling can be achieved using a two-prong centre providing it is driven into the material with a mallet before mounting in the lathe. When the work is reversed, a tapered plug is used to centre the work for the final drilling operation. After drilling, a second tapered plug is used to support the work between centres whilst the flange for the cap is made.

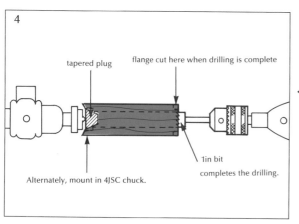

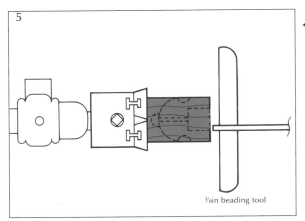

5

¾in beading tool

The body is now fitted to the cap and the bottom of the body is supported by a tapered plug in the tailstock. Cap and body are run together and shaped and finished together to give perfect alignment. Care should be taken to ensure that the length of the grinder mechanism has the correct protrusion from the top of the cap when turned down to a finish. Sand and finish in the normal manner. This can either be an oiled finish or a polished finish as required.

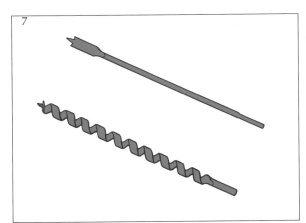

7

The illustration shows the alternative shapes of pepper and salt mills. It should be noted that pepper mills have stainless steel mechanisms, while salt mills have mechanisms made of durable nylon to resist corrosion. There is also available a chilli pepper mechanism, with which a glass body is recommended.

The cap is now mounted on the lathe either in a screw chuck, or in a scroll chuck. The centre is partly drilled to accept the grinder shaft (¼in drill bit) and the face is recessed with a parting tool as shown to fit the flange on the mill body. Take care that the recess wall is both smooth and vertical to ensure a good sliding fit.

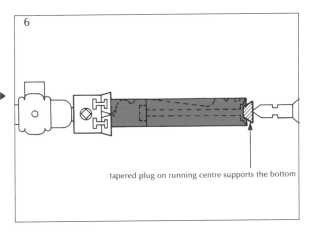

6

tapered plug on running centre supports the bottom

In the case of longer pepper mills, up to 18in, either a long auger bit or an extended shank flat bit has to be used. Both are illustrated. Auger bits are available in 10mm and 12mm diameter, at 16in length. Extended shank flat bits are available from 6mm to 25mm diameter, 15¾in long. Extension bars can be made up to saw tooth bits, and although they look promising, experience shows that they are seldom satisfactory.

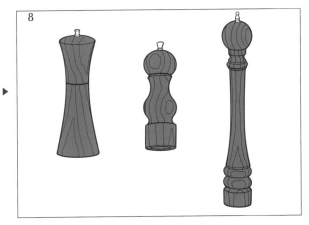

8

The salt and pepper shakers illustrated differ from the usual pattern in that they are based on a sixteenth-century pattern of spice shaker. They do not depend upon an inserted plastic plug in the base, but upon a carefully fitted flanged joint in the centre of the shaker. The method of turning follows that explained on pages 72 and 73, where a duplex chuck is used to produce hollow-ware by arranging for both the top and bottom of the article to be held independently in compression on the face of chuck.

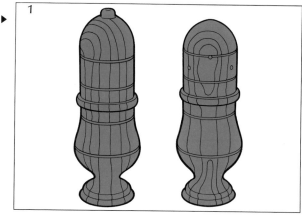

1

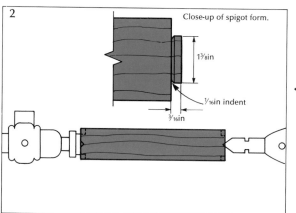

2

Close-up of spigot form.

$1\frac{3}{8}$in

$\frac{1}{16}$in indent

$\frac{3}{16}$in

The work is placed between centres and taken down to a cylinder with the roughing gouge. Both ends are trued with a skew chisel and $\frac{3}{16}$in spigots are cut at each end with an undercut to accommodate the chuck jaws in compression. Although only $\frac{1}{16}$in deep, this undercut is important to the correct functioning of the jaws.

Offer up both ends of the work to ensure that the chuck will grip on either end. Remove the tailstock and clamp the work firmly in compression in a Masterchuck. Set out the work as shown, part through the parting line between the top and bottom of the shaker, and put the top on one side.

3

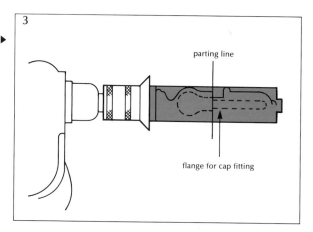

parting line

flange for cap fitting

4

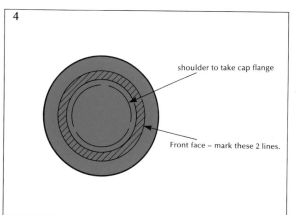

shoulder to take cap flange

Front face – mark these 2 lines.

Mark out the face of the base for hollowing with a $\frac{3}{8}$in and a $\frac{1}{4}$in gouge. Shape the internal curve with a left-hand cutting scraper working from the bottom of the recess upwards to the rim. This should be treated as a light finishing cut, the bulk of the work having already been done by the gouges.

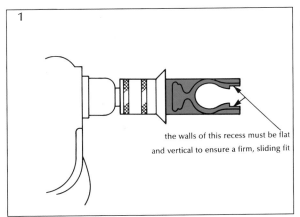

the walls of this recess must be flat
and vertical to ensure a firm, sliding fit

Ensure that the top ½in of the bottom recess is vertical by using a ½in skew chisel to produce a smooth finish. The exterior of the bottom can be shaped with a ⅜in and a ¼in gouge. The work should be sanded, decorated and finished in either wax or oil and removed from the chuck but not yet parted off. Do not sand the top ½in of the recess.

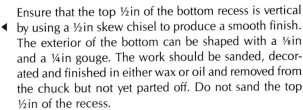

Mount the top section in a Masterchuck, take a careful reading of the aperture of the bottom of the shaker, and cut the inserted flange as shown with a parting tool and ⅜in beading tool. Leave a little material in hand (for example ¹⁄₁₆in on diameter) to allow for fine fitting with the beading tool.

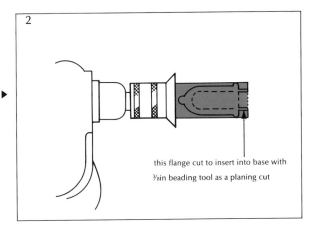

this flange cut to insert into base with
⅜in beading tool as a planing cut

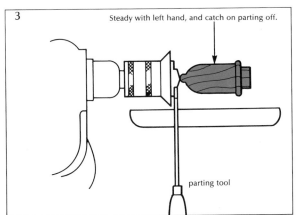

Steady with left hand, and catch on parting off.

parting tool

Test frequently for a tight sliding fit as soon as the base starts to run onto the flange. All fitting thereafter must be with the work stationary or there may be a danger of burning the flanges in contact. When a satisfactory sliding fit has been cut with the ⅜in beading tool, shape the exterior with the ⅜in bowl gouge and skew chisel, leaving a ¼in spigot at the headstock end. Sand, decorate and finish and finally part off at the ¼in spigot.

Re-mount the base in the chuck, mount the top of the shaker into the base, and finish the sanding and polishing where the spigot had been holding. If the shaker is required for salt, drill a ⅛in hole centrally in the top; if it is required for pepper, five holes of ¹⁄₁₆in diameter should be drilled in the nose.

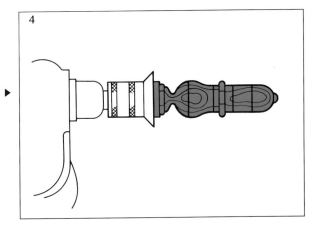

Place a square blank in a scroll chuck and rough down to a cylinder supported by the tailstock. Move the tailstock away and insert the Jacob's chuck fitted with a ⅝in saw-tooth bit. True the end of the work with ½in skew chisel and then drill with the ⅝in bit to ¼in. ▶

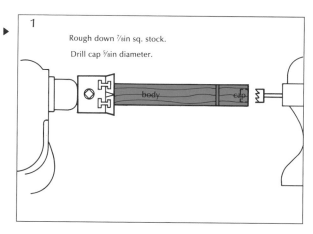

1

Rough down ⅞in sq. stock.

Drill cap ⅝in diameter.

body   cap

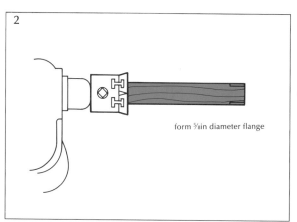

2

form ⅝in diameter flange

◀ Part the cap from the work with a junior hack-saw, form the flange on the end to suit the cap. This should be a tight sliding fit as in step 7, page 103. This sliding fit is achieved by using the ⅜in beading tool in a planing cut to give a mating surface which has no taper, and also to give a fine finish.

With the flange for the cap completed, place the drill in the tailstock with a ½in twist-bit and drill the remainder of the case to depth. With the tailstock moved out of the way re-fit the lid and turn both body and lid true with a ⅜in beading tool running as a planing cut. ▶

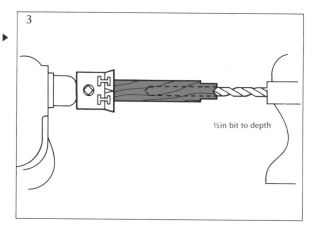

3

½in bit to depth

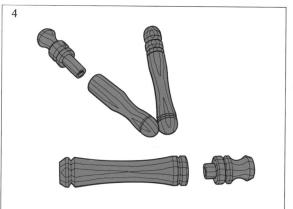

4

◀ Shape, decorate and finish the work to the required pattern. Part off from the headstock end using a junior hack-saw. A slimmer pattern could be turned using small drill bits, such as ½in for the cap and ⅜in for the body. An alternative and more tightly fitted cap can be made using a hollow plug sliding into the body.

The illustration shows a pole lathe which operates from a treadle, and has three turns around the tailstock to drive the bowl blank. Typical of these old treadle lathes, the drive axis is high (at chest height) and the rest higher still (at shoulder height). The tool is a hook tool, and used horizontally; the wood should be newly felled and full of sap.

The straight-stemmed hook tool is used to deepen and widen the grooves, marking out the three bowls so that it has free clearance. Progressively more curved hook tools are used which deepen and undercut the bowl profiles. At this stage, the turner cannot see the cutting edge of the hook and relies upon the feel of the tool only.

In a modern lathe with continuous motion, a nest of bowls of this size is not possible. The intermittent motion of the pole lathe allows for shavings to be ejected on the up-stroke. When the curved slots are completed, the work is removed from the lathe and the bowls forcibly detached from each other by splitting at the base, along the grain.

The under-surfaces of the bowl are turned flat and both the interior and exterior surfaces are finished. Care must be taken that the bowls do not dry too rapidly and crack. A common method was to immerse the newly turned bowls in their own wet shavings and then set aside them to dry slowly.

The amount of wood needed to complete these pens is so little that exotic woods are usually used in fashioning the upper and lower barrel. Blanks are cut to ⅜in square and drilled with a ¼in drill bit. Of the English hard-woods, walnut provides an admirable colour and finish.

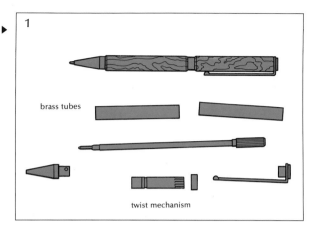

brass tubes

twist mechanism

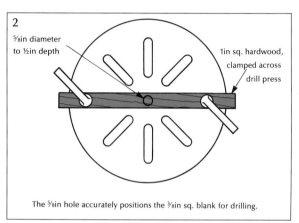

⅝in diameter to ½in depth

1in sq. hardwood, clamped across drill press

The ⅝in hole accurately positions the ⅜in sq. blank for drilling.

To assist in drilling the blank accurately, a jig will be found to be useful when using a pillar drill. For glueing the brass tubes into the drilled blanks, the suppliers recommend an instant glue, however, hot-melt glue or PVA resin W will work as well.

The recommended method of mounting the blanks for turning, as suggested by Craft Supplies of Derbyshire, is as follows:

'We suggest using the mandrel mounting kit which consists of two short brass tubes to mount at each end of the blanks. The outer diameter of the brass tubes is equal to the finished diameter of the pen and therefore acts as a very good guide as to when to stop removing wood.'

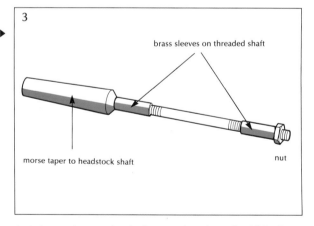

brass sleeves on threaded shaft

morse taper to headstock shaft

nut

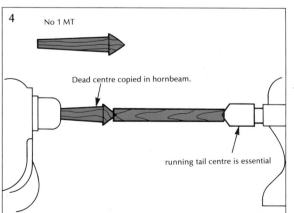

No 1 MT

Dead centre copied in hornbeam.

running tail centre is essential

An alternative method of mounting the tubed blanks is to prepare a No. 1 MT dead centre in a hardwood such as hornbeam, and load the work directly onto the wooden driving head and the running tailcentre. This provides quicker loading and unloading. The wooden drive head does not damage the brass tube, and still provides plenty of motive force.

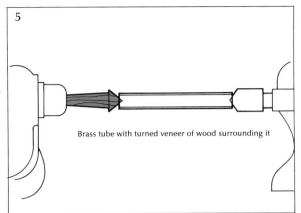

5

Brass tube with turned veneer of wood surrounding it

However the work is mounted, it is turned with a ⅜in bowl gouge to bring it to a round and then smoothed using a planing cut with a ⅜in beading tool. It is sanded in the usual way. There is insufficient veneer to permit any cut decoration. If this is to be attempted, then a thicker and possibly shaped veneer will be necessary.

The most suitable finish for this article is Craftlac melamine, again marketed by Craft Supplies of Derbyshire, which gives a high gloss finish to the wood in keeping with its function, and enabling it to withstand constant handling. A finishing touch, whether the pen is for sale or presentation, is a clear-fronted, black cardboard box, made to take the pen.

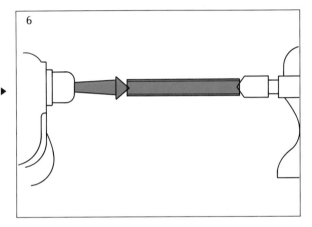

6

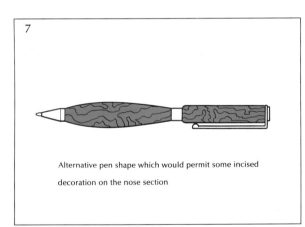

7

Alternative pen shape which would permit some incised

decoration on the nose section

Full instructions for assembly are given by the suppliers. Assembly is quite straightforward. Refills are readily available for these ball pens. The point retracts when the top of the pen is twisted. Craft Supplies also supply alternative patterns such as pencils and fountain pens, and a novel capped ball-point pen in the shape of a baseball bat.

There are also available pen blanks in a large variety of exotic woods. These blanks measure 6in in ½in sq. They are cut in half for drilling and turning, thus guaranteeing the continuity of the grain along the two halves. The blanks are supplied in packs of ten.

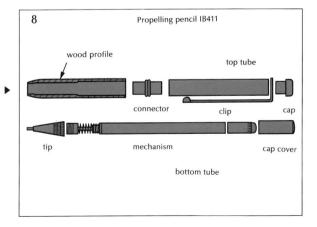

8   Propelling pencil IB411

wood profile

top tube

connector   clip   cap

tip   mechanism   cap cover

bottom tube

Two different woods should be chosen for the opposing sets of chessmen, such as hornbeam and rosewood. If it is necessary to make the two sets in one wood only, then one of them should be ebonized. The square work is mounted directly into a scroll chuck. Only two chess pieces require carving in addition to turning – the king and the knight.

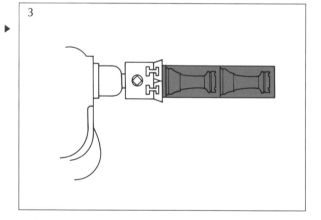

1

3 X 1¼in   2¾ X 1¼in   1⅝in X 1¼in   2 X 1¼in   2¼ X 1½in   1½ X ¾in

The king and queen are made from an 8in blank held in the scroll chuck brought down to a cylinder by a ⅜in bowl gouge and set out to the pattern as shown. The cross on the king's crown is turned as a ball and later sawn to shape. The queen's crown is later shaped with a narrow round file.

2

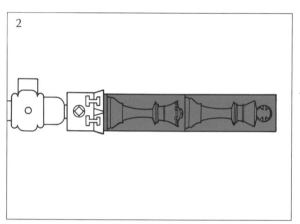

Two castles are turned, from a single 6in blank, to the pattern shown in the illustration. Sawcuts complete the battlements for these castles. To avoid difficulty in remounting the pieces for polishing or ebonizing, it is recommended that the first castle in the pair is plain polished to become the 'white' piece, and the second in the pair ebonized when turned, and polished before parting off.

3

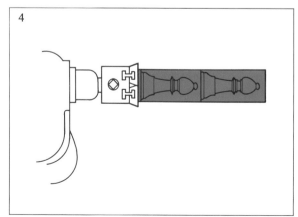

4

In the same manner, two bishops are made from a single 6in blank to the dimensions shown on the pattern stick. Diameters are found with the callipers and parting tool, and then the pieces are shaped using a ¼in LS deep-fluted gouge and the ⅜in beading tool. The bead work is cut with the toe of the ½in skew chisel. The slot for the bishop's mitre is cut with a saw after the work is removed from the lathe.

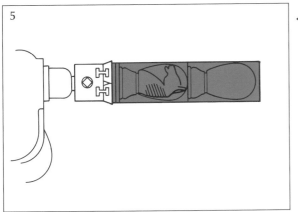

The knights are cut from wider stock, as a pair, and handcarved to the pattern shown after the base has been turned between centres. The same procedure as before is followed in polishing and ebonizing after carving, but in this case the finish will have to be by hand-polishing.

Four pawns can be made from one blank – a total of eight for each side will be needed. Care should be taken that these pawns are identical in shape and height and that they match the opposing set of pawns. They are turned in a similar manner to the bishops (*see* page 108, step 4). Diameters are found with callipers and parting tool, and the bulk of the waste removed with the ⅜in beading tool. Base detail and the collar are formed with the skew.

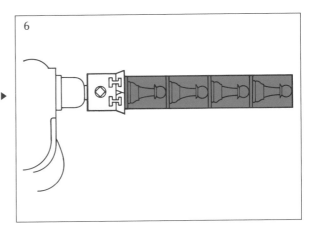

An alternative pattern of chessmen is shown in a rather more elaborate pattern. It may seem attractive to glue felt discs under all the chess pieces, but the felt will become worn and marked in a surprisingly short time. The smooth, slightly dished base presents a more serviceable and professional finish.

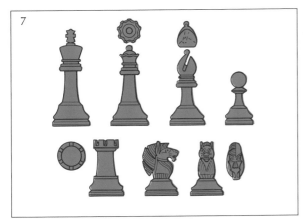

The chessboard itself should be made in the same two contrasting woods. If, instead of this, ebonizing is chosen as an alternative to a second wood, Liberon provide an excellent black polish, three coats of which will adequately ebonize these chessmen and the necessary parts of the board.

These dice can be made any size between 1in and 6in side, but 3in seems to give the most suitable handling. A length of 14in of hardwood is carefully planed square to 3in on all four faces. Circles of 3in diameter are scribed on the face of the work (with sufficient space between the circles to allow for parting) using the band-saw. Four dice will be made from one blank. ▶

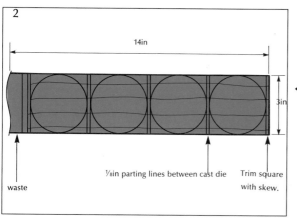

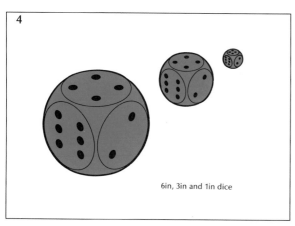

A 1in skew chisel is used to round the corners of the dice in exactly the same way as it is used to form a V-notch. The work should be stopped frequently to check that the chisel is conforming to the scribed circles on the blank. ◀

A ⅜in beading tool is used to finish the curves for the corners and also to round the edges of all four blanks. The rounded edges are important if the dice are to roll properly. ▶

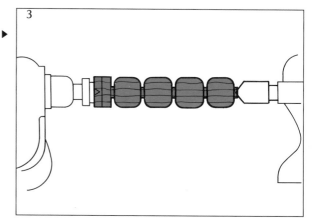

The dice are best painted in their strip of four before parting off in the band-saw. Two coats of white undercoat and a coat of gloss paint will be adequate. After parting off, the cut ends are sanded and similarly painted. Self-adhesive black discs are stuck on as the counting dots on all six faces. ◀

6in, 3in and 1in dice

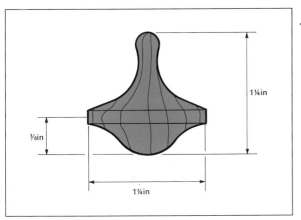

These are popular, easily made items and two methods are illustrated for turning these spinners. The first one uses a scroll chuck to mount the work between centres. Turning to a cylinder with the roughing gouge, set out the work as shown and then move the tailstock away to allow the spinners to be turned and parted off in succession.

A ¼in gouge is used to turn the spinners separately. Each is sanded and decorated, if required, with a ½in skew chisel, finished and parted off. A suitable finish would be sanding sealer, which is rubbed down briefly with wire wool, and then burnished with wood shavings for a few seconds.

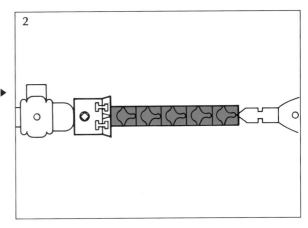

2

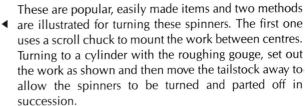

3

waste

An alternative method of production is to use a screw chuck, roughing out between centres as before. The work is set out in pencil and the tailstock moved away. The screw chuck should have a large screw fitted since it will have to hold in end-grain. No more than five finger spinners should be attempted in one piece of work.

The base of the spinner is formed with a ¼in bowl gouge and the waste removed to form the stem with the same tool. After sanding, the stem is parted off and the top itself is finished with two coats of polyurethane polish.

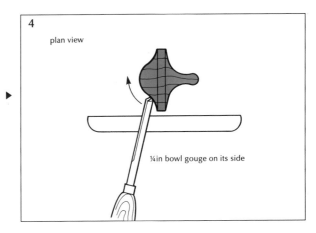

4

plan view

¼in bowl gouge on its side

The ring box is made from a wood blank cut down the middle as shown, so that the top and bottom halves of the ring box have matching grain. Both halves are then drilled right through using a ¼in drill bit for fitting to the Masterchuck, fitted with the screw chuck. Both blanks are cut to size on a band-saw. ▶

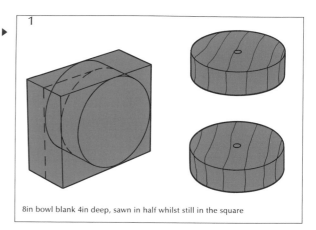

1

8in bowl blank 4in deep, sawn in half whilst still in the square

◀ The outside base of the ring box is formed using a beading tool and bowl gouge. The inside is formed using a ⅜in bowl gouge, the centre being left flat. All parts accessible are then sanded and finished and the base is removed from the screw chuck, reversed, and re-mounted in the same chuck.

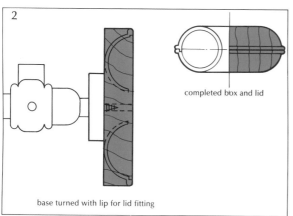

2

completed box and lid

base turned with lip for lid fitting

The outside of the base can now be finished using a ⅜in bowl gouge, a ⅜in beading tool and a skew chisel. Before finally parting at the centre of the ring box, sand and finish completely all that is accessible. Part off in the centre aperture using a diamond-shaped parting tool. ▶

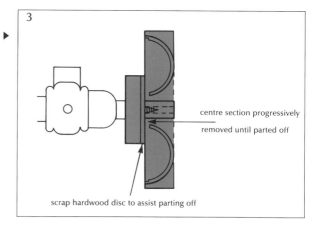

3

centre section progressively

removed until parted off

scrap hardwood disc to assist parting off

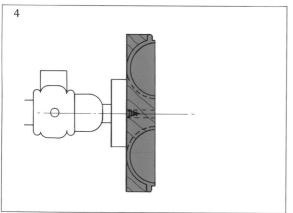

4

◀ Mount the lid blank. Use the bowl gouge and beading tool to form the outside curve and the bowl gouge to hollow out the inside of the lid. Callipers are placed across the base aperture to gauge the lip requirement for a tight-fitting lid. The lip from the lid should fit inside the bottom of the ring bowl. Sand and finish all parts of the ring box that are accessible.

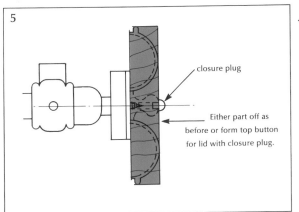

Reverse the lid of the ring box and use the bowl gouge, beading tool and skew chisel to complete turning the top of the lid, either leaving a button by which the top can be lifted, or a hole matching the hole in the base. Sand and finish off before either parting off or removing the top from the chuck.

Turn a tapered mandrel to accept the hole in the centre of the ring box top to permit final finishing. The taper on this mandrel should be gradual in order to allow a firm fit. An alternative method of mounting either the top or bottom of the ring box, for finishing, would be on expanding/contracting wood jaws as shown.

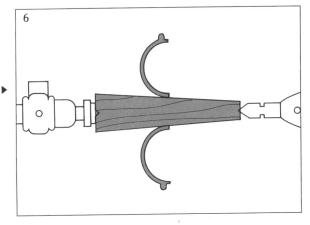

Mount the bottom of the ring box to either the tapered mandrel or the expanding wood jaws for final finishing. Note that with the tapered mandrel only sanding and polishing will be possible. However, with expanding/contracting wooden jaws any necessary re-cutting of the whole can be undertaken.

Variations in the pattern of ring boxes are shown, probably the most convenient being the ring box with the built-in button lid. This is a little easier to make than the pattern described on this page.

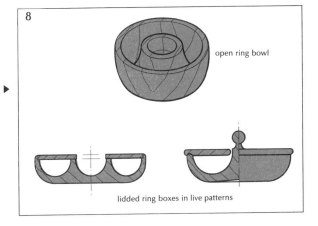

Time glasses vary in size from 3in to 20in in height. They may have three, four or five supporting spindles. The pattern illustrated is 5in high with a diameter of 2in, it has three spindles, and is a 4-minute time glass. The template for the end cap and the pattern bar for the spindle are shown. The wood should either be one of the exotics, since very little is used, or, if this is not chosen, any ebonized hardwood.

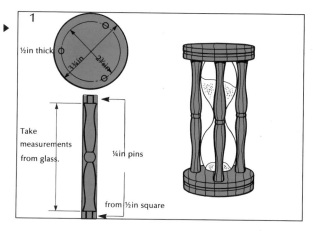

½in thick

3¼in   2½in

Take measurements from glass.

¼in pins

from ½in square

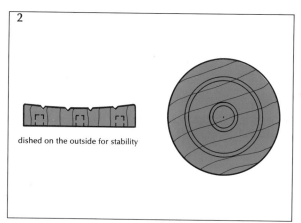

dished on the outside for stability

The end caps are band-sawed out, mounted on a screw chuck, brought to a round of 3¼in diameter and dished on the face. They are decorated with a skew chisel and finished in the usual way. Note that the screw chuck will only be required to penetrate ¼in into the work. Hardboard washers may be used to assist here, to reduce screw penetration.

With callipers, take the dimension of the time glass as shown, which will determine the length of the spindles between end caps. Dowels of ¼in will be turned at either end of the spindles. Use a dead centre to drive the spindle for ease of access to the end dowels.

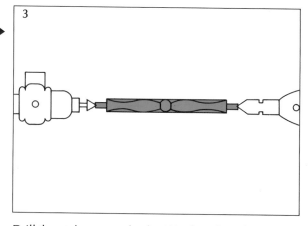

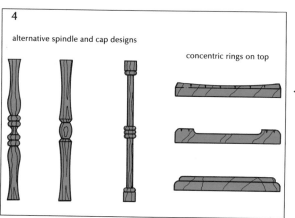

alternative spindle and cap designs

concentric rings on top

Drill the end caps to take the ¼in dowels and use a ½in drill bit to accommodate the end caps of the blown glass. Cut rubber discs from an old inner tube using a sharpened piece of pipe. Discs should be of ½in diameter and can be used to 'washer up' the end caps and provide a snug fit for the glass insert. When the fit is correct, glue, assemble and weight the spindles whilst the glue dries.

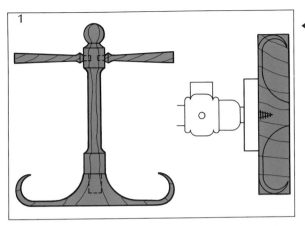

The central column is turned to pattern. Note that two diameters of ⅝in are made to assist drilling in the V-block. The central column has a ⅜in dowel to fit into the base.

This useful article provides a temporary home for rings that might otherwise get lost during the washing or other household chores. Turned in any hardwood, yew also gives a very good finish. The 3½in diameter base is band-sawed out and mounted on a screw chuck for hollowing with the bowl gouge as shown.

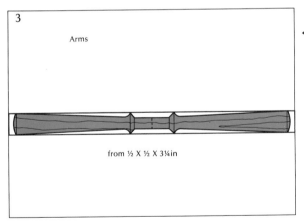

centre pin

⅝in diameter

from ¾ X ¾ X 3in

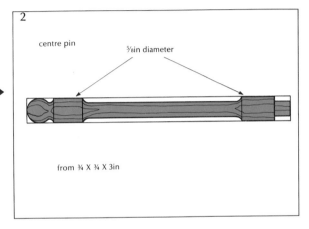

Arms

from ½ X ½ X 3¼in

The arms are made in one piece with waste at either end and a gauged ⅜in diameter at the centre to act as dowels for the centre column. All parts are finished in the usual way before parting off.

After a test assembly, glue and check for correct alignment. Alternatives to a ring tree are small ring stands that can be placed in the kitchen, bathroom or bedroom as required. The illustration shows two patterns of ring stand. These are conveniently turned using a screw chuck.

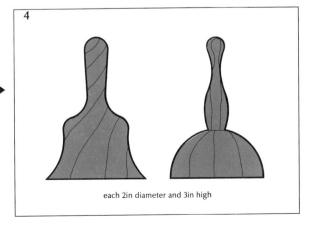

each 2in diameter and 3in high

The feature of this spinning disc is that the whorl is at the top of the dowel. The dowel is made from ⅜in commercially made ramin dowel and the disc diameter is 3¾in, 1in thick. The weight of the whorl is important to its function. In this example the whorl is made from elm.

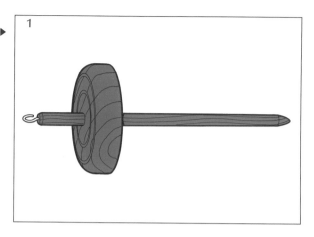

The disc is band-sawed and drilled through with a ¼in bit for fitting to the screw chuck on the Mastchuck. The disc is fitted to the chuck, the face trued and then reversed.

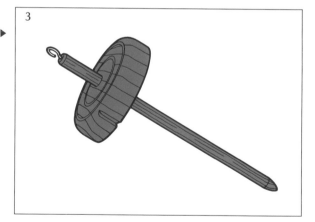

The disc is rounded, finished and decorated (a wax finish being preferred), and is completed by filing a V-notch in the rim through which the wool is led. The central hole is then enlarged to suit the dowel.

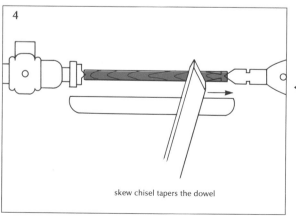

The cut section of dowel is mounted between centres and a skew is used to taper the point. Mount the dowel vertically in the vice and, with a hand drill, drill a hole to suit the ⅜in open hook which will be in the squared end. Allow for some adjustment of the disc on the dowel, but it should be a very tight sliding fit capable of being moved up the dowel only with some effort.

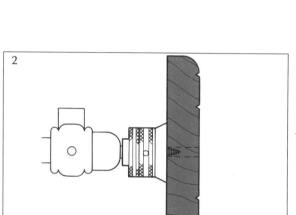

skew chisel tapers the dowel

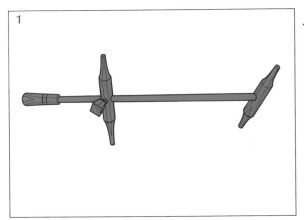

1

This piece of spinner's equipment is often referred to as a 'niddy-noddy' and, in use, it takes up the wool from the bobbin on the spinning wheel and winds it to a hank on the skein winder. Having produced the skein, the spinner is then able to wash, dye, or store the wool. This pattern has a movable bottom arm to facilitate removal of the hank, a feature not common to all skein winders.

The arms of the skein winder require holes drilled to fit the centre dowel and also the tap for threading the tensioning device on the bottom arm. All these holes are best drilled with the arms in the square. The hole for the handle is similarly drilled in the end of the handle in the square and then the handle is turned around the hole, thereby ensuring an accurate fit to the dowel. The tap used in the tensioning hole in the bottom arm is $\frac{5}{8}$ in and is drilled with a pilot hole of $\frac{9}{16}$ in.

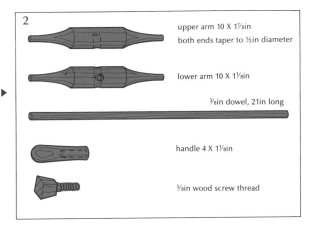

2

upper arm 10 X 1⅛in
both ends taper to ½in diameter

lower arm 10 X 1⅛in

⅜in dowel, 21in long

handle 4 X 1⅛in

⅝in wood screw thread

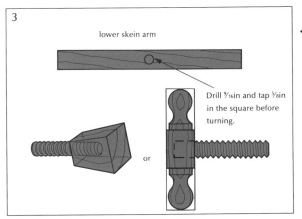

3

lower skein arm

Drill 9/16in and tap 5/8in in the square before turning.

or

The screw thread should be made from hornbeam or sycamore. Make a length of 3in and cut off to size. The nut can be square or round, or even a small butterfly, as required. Test assemble the skein winder and, if satisfactory, glue up.

In use, the skein winder takes up the wool from the bobbin in the manner shown in the illustration. Traditionally, one complete turn of the four sides of the skein winder should measure 2yd. When all the wool is wound onto the skein winder, the slider arm is moved upward and the hank taken off.

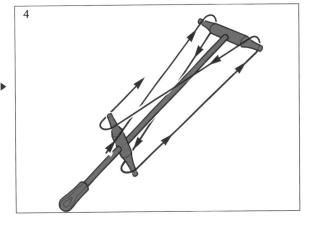

4

This equipment is used by lace-makers to wind cotton onto the neck of the lace bobbins used on lace pillows. The material used can be any hardwood. Ideally, the wood should match the lace horse and stool described on pages 121–123. ▶

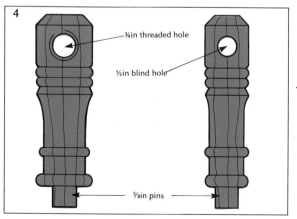

The baseboard is made from material not less than 1in ◀ finished thickness, planed flat on both sides and drilled as illustrated with six holes using a ⅝in saw-tooth bit.

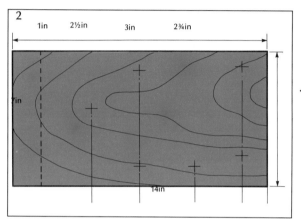

The cotton skein holder consists of two copy-turned uprights, pegged into the board and standing 2½in ▶ above the board. These are drilled to accept a ¼in length of ramin dowel on which the cotton skein can easily revolve.

The bobbin support and adjustment posts stand 4½in ◀ above the baseboard and are pegged into it with a ⅝in dowel. The right-hand post is through-drilled, when in the square, to accept a ¾in tap, and this threading is done before the post is turned. A ½in hole is drilled as shown on the left-hand post at the same height as the centre of the tapped hole. This will accept the nose of the bobbin, the head of the bobbin being carried on the threaded adjusting spindle. Both holes should have a felt disc to protect the bobbin.

Figure 4 labels:
- ¾in threaded hole
- ½in blind hole
- ⅝in pins

Figure 2 labels:
- 1in, 2½in, 3in, 2¾in
- 7in
- 14in

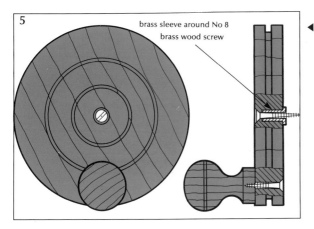

The main crank wheel is turned from ¾in wood of 5in diameter and has a ¼in slot for the driving band. Holes are drilled for the centre screw mounting and the turned handle at the rim. The post is turned in the normal way and drilled to accept a 1½in No. 8 screw.

The jamming ledge is screwed underneath the baseboard, which is then sanded and finished with paste wax to match the posts and wheel. It is sensible to fit felt underneath the baseboard to avoid scratching table surfaces.

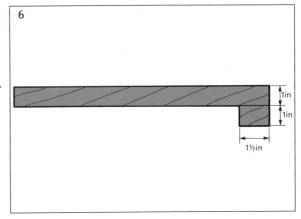

The bobbin container is an optional extra which provides a receptacle for bobbins which have been loaded with cotton. The crank wheel will require a small brass sleeve to allow easy running over the No. 8 brass screw which fits the wheel to the post.

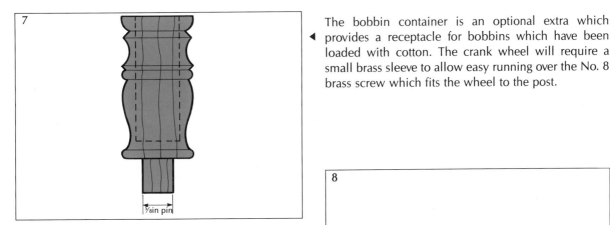

Torchon bobbins have spangles at the nose to tension the cotton. These require an attachment as shown to permit the spangles to spin freely when the bobbin is taking up the cotton. This attachment is turned from matching hardwood on a screw chuck.

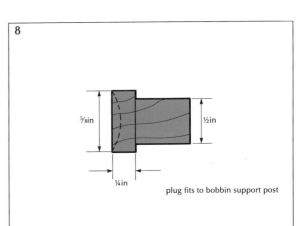

The main feature of the spinner's chair is the narrow back to permit free use of the arms when working a spinning wheel. This is a traditional feature of these chairs.

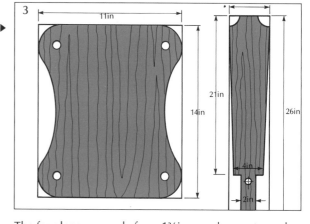

The choice of wood should be to match the spinning wheel, if possible. Failing that, the chair should be of elm in the seat and back and ash in the legs. The back is made of 1in material planed on both faces.

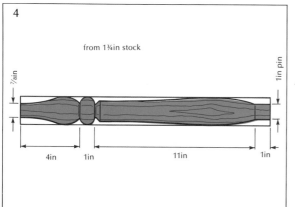

The seat is also made from 1in wood. The leg holes are angled as explained in step 4, page 88 with the exception that the holes are through-drilled. The legs, when fitted, are given a wedge in contrasting-coloured wood to ensure a firm fit in the seat.

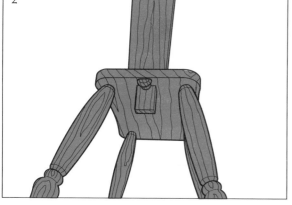

The four legs are made from 1¾in wood, copy turned as explained on pages 85 and 86. The length of the leg must be found by fitting the spinner to the wheel so that, when sitting comfortably, the elbow is at the exact height of the orifice on the flier. The chair is best finished in a paste wax and burnished.

1

This antique pattern dates from around 1800, and the wood used in its construction should match the lace horse detailed on pages 122 and 123 below. If it is not intended for use with a lace horse then, traditionally, the seat should be of elm, the legs and stretchers of ash. The finish should be wax, the legs having a spun finish and the seat being polished with paste wax.

The seat is made of 1½in material and is best cut using a card template which will also position the drilled holes for the legs. After band-sawing to shape, it is necessary to take a deep chamfer under the seat by angling the table on the band-saw. This chamfer is necessary to avoid the 'top-heavy' look which would otherwise arise from the deep material used.

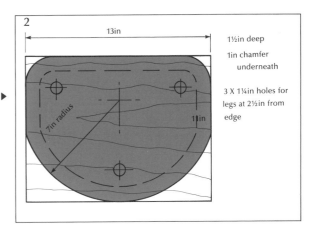

2

13in

1½in deep

1in chamfer underneath

3 X 1¼in holes for legs at 2½in from edge

7in radius

1in

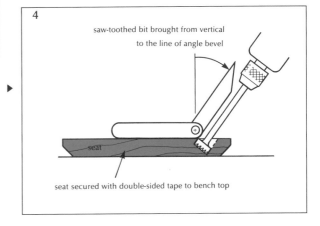

3

1½in

1½in

¾in

2¾in · 1in · 1¼in · 8in · ½in · 1¼in · 1¾in

¼in · ¼in · ¼in · 1in · pin

from 19 X 1¾in sq.

The three legs are copy turned in the usual manner; they are not through-fitted to the seat. The stretchers are copied using the pattern stick illustrated. All are finished with sanding sealer, wire wool, burnished and waxed.

The seat is drilled for the three legs, using either a sliding bevel or a pillar drill tilted to angle (*see* page 88). A saw-tooth bit is preferred for this operation, although it will be necessary to start the drill upright and at right angles to the work in order to let the bit settle in. Thereafter, the bit can be angled progressively down until the desired angle is reached. With the work clamped to an angled pillar drill, this process will not be necessary.

4

saw-toothed bit brought from vertical to the line of angle bevel

seat

seat secured with double-sided tape to bench top

The lace horse illustrated is not a traditional pattern, but one that was developed for the Honiton Lace Shop of that town on request. The original lace horses were of light strip material designed to fold flat and could not be considered attractive pieces of furniture. This lace horse forms the logo of my woodturning business and is unique to Devon Woodcrafts. The lace horse provides an interesting piece of furniture, is a convenient stand for a lace pillow and its lace and carries a working light, a bobbin tree, or a pin table.

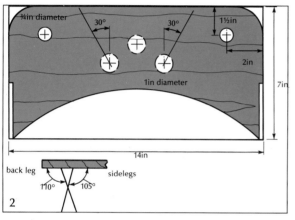

Band-saw the table and drill vertical ¾in holes to accept the light, bobbin tree, or pin table. On the underside of the table three holes, angled as shown, should be drilled to 1in diameter, not through-drilled.

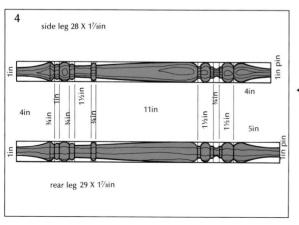

Sycamore (a 1¼in by ¼in strip), should be soaked in water for twenty-four hours and then placed in a former, as shown, to bend to fit to the lace horse table.

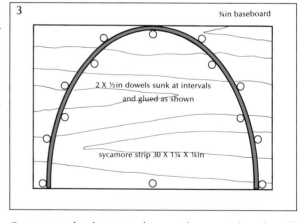

Copy turn the legs, as shown; the exact length will depend upon the lace-maker, who needs to work on the pillow at a comfortable height. An average length is shown for guidance.

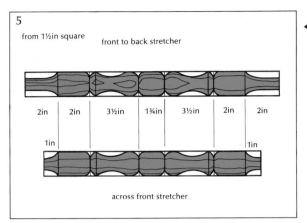

5

from 1½in square

front to back stretcher

| 2in | 2in | 3½in | 1¾in | 3½in | 2in | 2in |

1in   1in

across front stretcher

The stretchers are copy turned in the usual manner. ◄ Their length will, to some extent, depend upon the length of the legs. This can be ascertained as soon as the legs are mounted in the holes in the lace horse table.

The pin table is best turned on a screw chuck, should have a smoothed, dished top and the threaded upright ► dowelled into it. A threaded nut is tapped to ¾in diameter and fitted below the table to lock the pin table. Blocks to support the lace pillow are cut on the bandsaw. These are best produced by making a small cardboard template (at least three will be required).

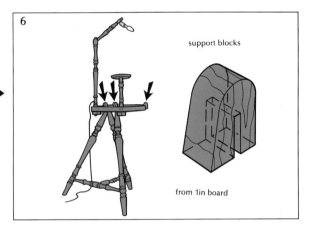

6

support blocks

from 1in board

7

The bobbin tree is self-explanatory and contains the ◄ threaded section in the same manner as the pin table, with a fixing nut to mount below the lace horse table. The light attachment can be drilled using the long-hole boring auger in the square, by sections, before being turned and assembled.

The polished components are test assembled and, if satisfactory, are glued. The lace pillow will fit into the ► hoop of sycamore and be supported by the blocks. The adjustable light can be mounted on the lace horse table and the bulb should be given a coat of heat-resisting paint (exhaust manifold silver is advised) on the side nearest to the lace-maker in order to shield the eyes from glare.

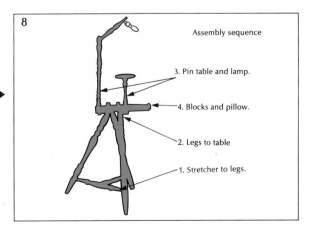

8

Assembly sequence

3. Pin table and lamp.

4. Blocks and pillow.

2. Legs to table

1. Stretcher to legs.

1 Hazardous Woods

The following list published by the *Woodworker* magazine in June 1990 gives a guide to woods producing irritant dusts.

Wood	Skin and eye allergies	Respiratory ailments
arbor vitae	—	X
ayan	X	—
beech	—	XXX
birch	—	X
blackwood (African)	X	—
boxwood (S. American)	X	X
cashew	X	—
cedar (western red)	X	XXX
cocobolo	X	X
cocus	X	—
dahoma	—	X
dogwood	—	X
ebony	X	X
greenheart	X	X
guarea	—	X
ipe	X	X
iroko	X	XXX
katon	—	X
mahogany (American and African)	X	X
makore	X	X
mansonia	XXX	X
maple	—	XXX
myrtle	—	X
obeche	X	X
opepe	X	X
peroba (rose and white)	X	X
pine	—	X
ramin	—	X
redwood	—	XXX
rosewood (Brazilian)	X	X
rosewood (E. Indian)	X	X
satinwood (Sri Lankan)	X	—
satinwood (W. Indian)	XXX	—
sequoia redwood	—	X
sneezewood	—	X
sucupira	X	—
teak	X	XXX
wenge	X	X

2 Turning Speeds

Diameter of Workpiece	Theoretical Revs for 25ft per second	Likely Available Revs Per Minute	
		Startrite Graduate	Tyme Avon
½in	11,457	2,250	2,000
1in	5,725	2,250	2,000
2in	2,864	2,250	2,000
3in	1,909	2,250	2,000
4in	1,431	1,330	2,000
5in	1,154	1,330	1,150
6in	954	1,330	1,150
7in	815	790	750
8in	716	790	750
10in	572	790	470
12in	477	425	470
18in	318	425	470

The table is based on the peripheral speed of the work. As cuts are made nearer to the centre of the work, for example in bowl turning, the cutting speed will be markedly reduced.

3 Tool Identification Numbers

Since my tools are all stored blade down, it is necessary to colour code and number the handles for ease of recognition. This is my personal numbering system, and is not nationally recognized.

Tool Number	Description
1	1½in roughing gouge
2	½in skew chisel
3	1in skew chisel
4	¼in LSDF bowl gouge
5	⅜in LSDF bowl gouge
6	½in LSDF bowl gouge
7	⅛in beading tool
8	¼in beading tool
9	⅛in diamond-shaped parting tool

4 Screw Threading

The female thread is cut with the steel tap provided with the screw box set. A pilot hole is drilled as follows.

For Tap Size	Pilot Hole
½in	⅛in
⅝in	$\frac{7}{16}$in
¾in	$\frac{9}{16}$in
1in	¾in
1¼in	1in
1½in	$1\frac{3}{16}$in

(With acknowledgements to the Lion Tool Company)

5 Pyrography Equipment

JANIK EQUIPMENT

Models G and G4 with:
(a) Decorative brands (1–12)
(b) Standard Points   (2 patterns)

HOT WIRE PYROGRAPH

This uses heavy-duty heated wire which is shaped to the user's requirements.

6 Lace Bobbins

LACE BOBBIN BLANKS

Packs of ten, twenty or fifty ⅜in square 6in long, from John Boddy's Fine Wood and Tool Store,
Boroughbridge
YO5 9LJ.

DECORATED LACE BOBBINS

Biggins Bobbins – Lace-Making Equipment
1 Archery Close
Cliffe Woods
Rochester ME3 8HN

Christine and David Springett
121 Hillmorton Road
Rugby CV22 5DF

Newham Lace Equipment
11 Dorchester Close
Basingstoke RG23 8EX

7 Abrasive Papers

Abrasive Papers				
Glasspaper	Garnet	Flint	Garnet Aluminium oxide Silicone carbide (wet and dry)	Emery
			400	
	9/0		320	
	8/0		280	
	7/0		240	
	6/0		220	0
00 (flour)				
0	5/0		180	
	4/0		150	
1	3/0	120	120	F
1½	2/0	100	100	
F2				1½
M2			60	2
S2				2½
2½	1½	1½	40	3
3	2	2	36	½
	2½	2½	30	4
	3	3	24	4½

8 Aide Memoire

Safety

Always check speed and rest firmness before starting.
Rotate by hand before starting.
Remove the rest before sanding/polishing.
Use a mask when cutting irritant woods, for example iroco or mahogany, and when bowl sanding.
Use a shield when grinding.

Tools

Roughing gouge; skew chisel; bowl gouge; beading tool; diamond-shaped parting tool.
Only put the weight of the tool on the grindstone.
Sharpen in line by rolling (gouges), and across by sliding (chisels).

Lathe Speeds

If 2in square or less, use 2,000 r.p.m. The larger the work, the lower the speed.
Bobbins – high speed; bowls – low speed.

Rules

Always turn from high to low.
Start taking off where the maximum must come off.
Keep the handle low and the bevel rubbing.

Sequence of Operation

In this order:
shaping
finishing
sanding
decoration

Single Chucking

Faceplate
Screws or double-sided tape.
Screw chuck.
Prepared flange for duplex multi-purpose chucks, or Jacob's chuck (between centres).

Double Chucking

First operation with:
faceplate
screw chuck
pin chuck
Second operation with:
duplex multi-purpose chucks
faceplate with 2in tape
Jacob's chuck

Decoration

V-notch or hot wire.
Carving or poker work.

Finishing

Sanding sealer, flat with steel wool, followed by Carnauba wax or 50/50 carnauba/beeswax; or Briwax with steel wool; or Danish oil x3.

Long-Hole Boring

Lowest speed.
Not more than 2in drilling each time.

When it Starts to go Wrong

Change some or all of these:
the tool, or sharpen it
the rest height or angle
the speed

Wood Usage

Ash – Impact resistant. Suitable for handles, stool and chair legs.
Elm – Will not split. Suitable for seat bottoms, kitchen utensils.
Sycamore – Close grained. Suitable for furniture, kitchenware and screw threads.
Oak – Good figure, stable. Ideal for furniture.
Chestnut – As oak.
Hornbeam – Heaviest UK wood. Used for mallet heads, skittle balls and screw threads.
Beech – Close grained. Good for furniture and screw threads.
Yew – Hard, inclined to splinter, takes a high polish. Suitable for furniture and small turned items.
Pine – Soft. Furniture and bannisters.
Holly – Close-grained, almost white. Ideal for lace bobbins.